'Don't Delay - Enrol Today'

'Don't Delay - Enrol Today'

# The WOMEN'S LAND ARMY IN HAMPSHIRE

JOHN K. LANDER

The History Press

First published 2024

The History Press
97 St George's Place, Cheltenham,
Gloucestershire, GL50 3QB
www.thehistorypress.co.uk



British Library Cataloguing in Publication Data.
A catalogue record for this book is available from the British Library.

ISBN 978 1 80399 751 3

Typesetting and origination by The History Press.
Printed and bound in Great Britain by TJ Books Limited, Padstow, Cornwall.

MIX
Paper | Supporting responsible forestry
FSC® C013056
FSC www.fsc.org

Trees for Life

# Contents


Dedication 7
List of Illustrations 8
Abbreviations 10
Foreword 11
About the Author 13
Preface and Acknowledgements 14

**Part 1: First World War, 1914–1918** **17**
1: Introduction 19
2: Initial National Response to Labour Shortages on Farms 21
3: Hampshire's Responses to Labour Shortages on Farms up to 1916 25
4: The Women's Land Army from March 1917, Nationally and in Hampshire 38
5: Post-war Experience 52
6: Postscript 59

**Part 2: Second World War, 1939–1945** **63**
7: Introduction 65
8: Early Women's Land Army Training at the County Farm Institute, Sparsholt 67
9: Women's Land Army Members' Experience in Hampshire 1939–1942 75

10: Expansion of Women's Land Army in Hampshire, 1943–1945 97
11: Continuing Role for Women's Land Army After 1945 109
12: Conclusion 120

**Appendices** **123**
A: Profile of a Land Girl – Gwendoline (Gwen) Raggett (née Place) MBE 123
B: Hymn of the Hampshire Countryside 128
C: Two Poems Written by Isabella D.S. Waddell in 1941, Aged 22 129
D: Women's Land Army Uniform 131

Notes 132
Bibliography 143
Index 145

# Dedication

'*Don't Delay – Enrol Today*'[1] is dedicated to two unassuming but remarkable women who were members of the Women's Land Army in Hampshire. They epitomise the invaluable service given to the nation by tens of thousands of women and girls in land-based jobs in two world wars.

| | |
|---|---|
| Mary Elizabeth (Liz) Bridges (née Cheal) | 1929–2023 |
| Gwendoline (Gwen) Yvonne Raggett (née Place) | 1926– |

# List of Illustrations


*p.28* 'English girls learning the trade of farming to take the place of farmers who have gone off to war, Sparsholt, Hampshire, England, 26 April 1915. Here they are seen following the harrow.' (Getty Images, serial no. 167182537; Underwood Archives)

*p.29* Westley Farmhouse, Sparsholt, built circa 1870. (Sparsholt College)

*p.36* Romsey Remount Depot, Isolation Hospital (National archive catalogue no. WO161/117)
Memorial Statue in Romsey War Memorial Park, commemorating the work of the Romsey Remount Depot.

*p.39* William Palmer, 2nd Earl of Selborne, President, Board of Agriculture, 1915–1916. (Bassano Ltd, via Wikipedia)

*p.42* 'WOMEN wanted at Once FOR THE LAND'.
'The Women's Land Army needs YOU to-day'.

*p. 45* Women's Land Army Rally, Andover, 1916. (WLA website)

*p. 50* Certificate signed by Rowland Prothero and Arthur Lee.
Good Service Ribbon Badge (Land Army Agricultural Section).

*p.54* Certificate of Discharge on Demobilisation.

*p.56* *The Landswoman,* August 1919. The wording reads 'The future is in the hands of the woman: What will she sow?'

*p.71* Tractor driving. (Sparsholt College Library archive)
Ploughing with horses. (Sparsholt College Library archive)

*p.72* A Sparsholt bull. (Sparsholt College Library archive)
Horticultural students with the apple harvest. (Sparsholt College Library archive)

*p.77* 'Members of the Women's Land Army being instructed in the art of thatching.' (Getty Images, serial no. 1297440939; Photo by Reg Speller)

*p.80* Women's Land Army membership card issued to Isabella D.S. Waddell – 25 July 1940 (front and reverse).

*p.81* An 'Australian Sunshine Stripper harvester' being demonstrated at Mr W.H. Wroth's farm. Bunty Horniblow is the person standing on the machine. (Reproduced with thanks to Bruce and Gill Horn)

*p.83* Recruitment poster, 1941.
*p.85* 'The Land Army Growing Vegetables for the Navy', showing a gang of land girls harvesting and packaging cabbages into wooden crates with the Isle of Wight in the background. (Picture by Archibald Standish Hartrick, courtesy of the Garden Museum)
*p.86* Plan for 'Agricultural Workers' Hostel' at Colden Common, Brambridge, submitted to Winchester Rural District Council, 1 August 1941, approved 28 August 1941.
*p.87* Dining room at a Women's Land Army Hostel. (Painting by Evelyn Dunbar, 1943)
*p.90* Redenham House, Weyhill, Hampshire, circa 1945. (Lent by Redenham House staff)
Memorial tree in Redenham House grounds, planted by Gwen and Maurice Raggett.
Memorial plaque provided by Gwen Raggett in 1990, at the base of the tree.
*p.92* Hostel built for the land girls at Hale Nursery, near Fordingbridge.
Land girls in their familiar uniform at Hale Nursery, circa 1945.
*p.100* Timber Corps camp accommodation.
*p.103* Leaflet (1943) featuring Amelia King, issued to draw attention to racial discrimination.
Land girls at Frith Farm, Wickham, including Amelia King (circa 1944). (Wickham History Society)
*p.110* Land girls driving tractors at a Rally, Southampton, 1946.
*p.113* 'Release Certificate' for Jeanne Mason, 5 August 1947.
*p.117* Membership Card, Women's Land Army Old Girls Association, Hampshire and Isle of Wight; Mrs D. Bowman, 29 March 1951. (HRO ref; 50M90/6)
Final Reunion of Women's Land Army Old Girls' Association, Hampshire and Isle of Wight, 27 April 1968.
*p.119* Programme of the 'Hampshire Service of Thanksgiving to recognise the contribution made by members of the Women's Land Army and Women's Timber Corps', 7 May 2009.
*p.121* Women's Land Army and Women's Timber Corps Memorial. Unveiled by HRH Countess of Wessex, 21 October 2014. (Egghead06, CC BY-SA 4.0, Wikimedia Commons)
*p.126* Gwen Raggett, 1926, aged 17. (Copy supplied by GR)
*p.127* Land girls, and officials, in front of the main entrance to Redenham House, 1947. Gwen is seated on the ground, second in from the right. (Copy supplied by GR)
*p.130* Isabella D.S. Waddell in her Women's Land Army uniform.

# Abbreviations

| | |
|---|---|
| **NFU** | National Farmers' Union |
| **'War Ags'** | War Agricultural Executive Committee |
| **WI** | Women's Institute |
| **WLA** | Women's Land Army |
| **WNLSC** | Women's National Land Service Corps |
| **WDRC** | Women's Defence Relief Corps |
| **WTC** | Women's Timber Corps |

# Foreword

It is an honour to write a foreword to this book which highlights the tremendous commitment of some 240,000 women and girls who volunteered to join the Women's Land Army to work on farms, in market gardens, and forestry, during the two world wars. They gave up their jobs and homes, often in urban areas, and left their families and friends for a life of manual work in the countryside. For many, this was a new work experience and lifestyle: milking cows, driving tractors, mucking out pigs, hauling timber with horses, and sleeping on bunk beds in hostels with basic facilities.

In making this personal sacrifice they helped boost the production of home-grown food and timber as part of the war effort to feed and support the nation. They responded to the nation's hour of need, and the nation owed them an everlasting debt.

John Lander, the author, undertakes research into local history. He leaves no stones unturned in the pursuit of detailed information, as I discovered in his discussions with me as a former Principal of Sparsholt College, Hampshire, when he was researching material for his book on the history of the college, *A Place of Transformation,* published in 2022. This same approach is evident in researching the WLA during both world wars, nationwide as well as in Hampshire. He has traced surviving land girls as well as relatives of others who were in the Land Army, gathering information about their experiences. One land girl revealed that she was given the responsibility of driving a 3-ton lorry, perhaps before her 18th birthday, and another described her wide variety of roles; potato picking, milking and harvesting sugar beet were examples.

The book presents a detailed account of the work and living conditions that the volunteer land girls experienced, as well as the demands they faced doing land work as their contribution to the war effort. Some were also confronted by other social, prejudicial and economic challenges. A few farmers were reluctant to employ women, some applicants experienced racism when applying to join the WLA, and the wages paid to land girls were below those paid to men for the same work. Nevertheless, land girls were lauded by many for the work and commitment they had shown in replacing male workers who had left for military service.

On reflection, it seems likely that WLA workers had a much wider impact on society beyond their efforts to boost food production. Women working in the First World War led to the opening of the labour market and, eventually, to equal voting rights. Land girls employed in the Second World War showed that they were quite capable of doing work traditionally done by men, and thereby strengthened the case for equal opportunities and equal pay in the land-based sector.

Following the final parade commemorating the WLA in 1950, the Queen said that 'the land girls had earned a noble share in the immense effort which carried our country to victory'. Details of that 'immense effort' are recounted in this book.

Dr Len Norman, PhD, MSc, BSc
Principal, Sparsholt College, 1970–1998

# About the Author

A banker by profession, though a social historian by natural inclination, most of John Lander's career was with one of the joint stock banks, culminating in an appointment as a Corporate Finance Director. He subsequently became a director of a publicly quoted company, and Director of Finance at an independent school.

In 1989, John embarked on Open University study, obtained a BA (Hons) and, following submission of a thesis entitled *Tent Methodism: 1814–1832,* was awarded a PhD in 2000. Since then, he has written over twenty-five books and papers published in specialist journals, mainly concerned with aspects of nineteenth- and twentieth-century Nonconformist Church history, and Cornwall's teetotal movement.

In retirement, John became a governor of Truro and Penwith College, where he chaired its Finance and General Purposes Committee, served as Chair of Coastline Housing Ltd, Vice Chair of Cornwall Rural Housing, and as a non-executive director of the Royal Cornwall Hospitals (NHS) Trust.

Since moving to Hampshire with his wife in 2019, John has become Chair of Winchester Housing Trust Ltd, a provider of social and affordable housing, and a church trustee. While he was a governor of the Sparsholt College Group he wrote the college's history, *A Place of Transformation,* which was published in 2022. It was while conducting the research for that book that John discovered the full extent of the Women's Land Army, and the significant part the college played in the training of land girls.

# Preface and Acknowledgements

One reason for writing about the Women's Land Army (WLA) now is that in November 2025 the country will mark the 75th anniversary of its demobilisation in 1950. Recording the work of thousands of women and girls on Hampshire farms, in not one but two world wars, will remind us that while, understandably, we can become preoccupied with day-to-day pressures, let alone recognise traumatic events around the world, there will be an opportunity to recall the vital contributions that women and girls made to wartime successes by maintaining food production.

I came to realise the full extent of the valuable assistance WLA members gave to Hampshire's farmers while researching and writing *A Place of Transformation*. From 1915 to 1918 and again from 1940 to 1944, the college's curriculum of one-year courses was abandoned, and staff devoted their expertise to training women and girls for tasks undertaken on Britain's farms.

Sparsholt College Library holds a wide range of primary material, Hampshire's Record Office has many archival documents, and local newspapers frequently reported WLA activities. Population censuses, particularly the September 1939 Registration, a family history website, and the 'Google' search engine, have all been useful. Books referring to the national impact the WLA had on the country's food production have been consulted. I have appreciated the assistance of the librarian at Sparsholt College for her ready willingness to help over several years, and for the cooperation of staff at Hampshire's Record Office, the *Hampshire Chronicle,* and the Museum of English Rural Life, part of the University of Reading.

Possibly the most rewarding aspect of writing this book has been the fruitful and fascinating conversations in the homes of descendants of people with WLA involvement. Material has been rescued from lofts and other places, and their enthusiasm and willingness to tell me of their links has been greatly appreciated. The book's endnotes make appropriate acknowledgement of the information they gave me. I'm grateful to the members of my family who gave me much needed help with IT matters and, yet again, to my wife for her support while I've been ensconced in my study, or out visiting record offices, libraries and people with stories to tell.

It is inevitable that as time goes by the number of former land girls able to impart their personal wartime experiences reduces. It has, then, been a moving privilege to meet with two elderly women who served in the WLA. In October 2022, I had a detailed discussion with a lady, born in 1929, who trained at Sparsholt and then worked as a land girl for several years from 1947. Elizabeth (Liz) Bridges (née Cheal), over lunch that she was determined to prepare, pressed me to write about the vital work undertaken by women in both world wars, and beyond. Sadly, Elizabeth died in August 2023, aged 94, and won't see the end result of her request. And then, in December 2023, I met with Gwen Raggett (née Place), 97 years of age, who recalled with great clarity some of the highlights of her six years as a land girl. Gwen and her daughter-in-law have huge volumes of preserved documents that have been made available to me. This book is dedicated to Gwen and Liz who, among countless women and girls, diligently served their country and the county of Hampshire in arduous wartime land-based jobs.

Another reason for describing the work of the WLA is that it 'is often referred to as the "Cinderella Service", a pillar of the war effort that was taken for granted and insufficiently recognised – both during the conflict and afterwards'.[1] Much more attention has been given to those women's organisations that were directly associated with the armed forces, such as the Auxiliary Territorial Service, the Women's Royal Navy Service, and the Women's Auxiliary Air Force. Far less acknowledged are the contributions of land-based employees, working very long hours, performing hard physical work in all weathers, and often a long way from their homes. This book is intended, in a modest way, to put right that inadequate recognition. This is especially so in the light of claims, made with some justification, that Hampshire might have been the first English county in both world wars to begin the training and placing of women and girls into agricultural settings.

# Part 1:

# First World War, 1914–1918

# 1

# Introduction

The contributions that WLA members made in maximising food production while large numbers of United Kingdom men served in the armed forces during the Second World War is universally acknowledged. Far less well known is that twenty-five years earlier the county of Hampshire was in the forefront of recruiting, training and placing women and girls in farms when it became clear that the First World War was not to be won within a few months. Many Hampshire residents, including prominent individuals, and staff at the Farm School, Sparsholt, played pioneering and crucial roles in addressing the urgent need to maximise home food production to offset reductions in imports.

The employment of women on farms in the period leading up to 1914 was not new. However, while the overall number of women in paid work nationally was steadily increasing, multiplying threefold between 1900 and the end of the war, that had not been the case in agriculture. At the time of the 1871 population census, 33,513 'girls and women were out-door agricultural labourers', nearly 25 per cent fewer than the 43,946 ten years earlier.[1] While the method of calculation probably changed over the decades, and comparison with previous censuses may be flawed, the extent of the decline was strikingly evident from the 1911 census statistics when just 13,245 females were recorded as 'agricultural labourers'. In that year, only 8 per cent of England's agricultural workers were female. Most of those were employed in the northern half of England, and a sense of the quite different position in southern counties can be gauged by knowledge that only 1 per cent of Hampshire's agricultural labourers were female.[2] As a detailed example, the 1911 population census showed that 2.6 per cent of all Hampshire labourers working in market gardens were female, but in Cheshire it was 17 per cent and in Lancashire 14.5 per cent.[3]

For many decades, there had been a growing reluctance of women to undertake arduous farm jobs. There was the 'gradual disengagement of women from agricultural labour ... under the impact of increasing mechanisation, specialisation, and the acceptance of the ideology of domesticity which frowned upon women's labour and especially physical work.'[4] A further factor was that wages paid to women employed on farms were normally less than half the rate paid to men, and substantially less than amounts earned by females in occupations in the more industrial parts of the country. The urgent need for women and girls to replace men on farms was prompted by three factors: the rapid enlistment of large numbers of men to join the armed services; significant reductions in quantities of imported food by sea; and the requisition of at least 600,000 horses that were the main source of power on farms, for transfer to the Western Front.

While single women were readily accepted as employees in many sectors, the subject of married women undertaking work in most capacities was controversial for many more years. 'Marriage bar' restrictions were lifted for the four war years because, by January 1915, 100,000 male agricultural labourers had already left to join the armed forces. They were, though, strictly reimposed in 1918 when widespread unemployment among men was predicted. The ban on married women teachers and BBC employees was lifted in 1944 but lasted for much longer in the civil service. While sustained pressures eventually led to the start of a steady process to allow women to take a greater share in contributing to the nation's gross domestic product, the Foreign Service did not allow married women as employees until 1973.

# 2

# Initial National Response to Labour Shortages on Farms

The First World War began on 4 August 1914. The grain harvests that year were expected to be excellent, and although many male farm labourers had already left their land-based jobs, no special need to employ more women had been identified. There was, though, encouragement for schoolboys aged between 11 and 14 to assist farmers in gathering crops during their summer holiday. By the end of the year, however, concern about labour shortages appeared. The campaign to attract more females to replace men began in earnest early in 1915, and continued spasmodically throughout the remaining war years. Even so, in 1915 and again in 1916, arrangements were made for serving soldiers to return to the United Kingdom for two weeks' furlough in the late spring and up to four weeks in the main harvesting season. In the first of those years, a total of 12,525 men took advantage of the opportunities to have a break from the fighting and help with haymaking and grain harvests, although farmers had sought 19,000.[1]

The WLA was not formally established until March 1917. Three years before then, it had been intended to hold a government-sponsored Agricultural Education Conference to determine what actions should be taken to maintain food production. In April 1914, a parliamentary question enquired how plans for the conference were progressing, and whether women were to be co-opted to its membership, bearing in mind that one topic related 'to women's rural education'.[2] The answer that the Board of Agriculture had still to appoint six more members suggested a strange lack of urgency given the deteriorating prospect of sufficient resources to maintain, let alone increase, home food production. The conference was finally held eight months later, in December 1914, but Lord Selborne, President of the Board of Agriculture, had to say in June 1915 that the official report of the meeting was still being prepared. Yet another eighteen months were to elapse before the WLA became a reality.

That delay did not prevent attempts by non-governmental bodies to attract women and girls to undertake general work on farms. A plethora of organisations emerged, mostly akin to present-day employment agencies, to recruit permanent farm employees, and others to help at peak times. Some were successful in persuading government to provide financial grants towards their initial costs, but otherwise no official support was forthcoming.

Among many organisations, the Women's Farm and Garden Union, established in 1899 as the Women's Agricultural and Horticultural International Union, had long advocated the benefits of limited female work on farms. In mid-1915, a year after the war began, the union reported that 'since the outbreak of war, a large number of trained women had been placed by the Union in gardens and in farms'.[3] Another body, the Women's Defence Relief Corps, was formed in September 1914. It had one section that was, from the spring of 1915, mainly involved in providing temporary labour to pick fruit, harvest the hop crop and haymaking. The corps offered to supply 'gangs of five or ten strong young women as harvesters'.[4] It was felt that providing the women were healthy and physically fit, only three days' training would be necessary, and that would be provided by the farmers for whom they worked. Although its advertising campaign sought to attract women, paying them a minimum of 18/- per week, the WDRC was constrained by shortage of funds, and had placed only 500 women by the summer of 1917. They came from a wide range of occupations, and most of them were living in London.[5]

One quasi-official organisation, set up in February 1916 after consultation with the Board of Agriculture, was the Women's National Land Service Corps, assisted by a £150 government grant towards formal training. In addition to requiring 'young, strong, educated women who can give their whole time … at ages between 18 and 35',[6] 2,000 volunteers were wanted to provide temporary help to farmers for short periods in the growing seasons. In April 1917, the 900 permanent members of the WNLSC were offered the chance to join the WLA, but, to the intense disappointment of the authorities, only eighty-eight accepted the invitation.[7] It seemed that while many women were prepared to undertake work for a few weeks in the spring and summer, they were not willing, or able, to commit for a longer period.

In the absence of official recognition, those efforts achieved only modest success. Perhaps recognising general irritation among people keen to move forward, Lord Selborne stressed in January 1916 that the employment of women was 'of the greatest consequence to agriculture' and that 'upon the solution of the question depends whether agriculture is or is not going to rise triumphantly over its difficulties'.[8] He was not the only senior government official to express frustration at delays in addressing the potential shortfall in food production. In May 1916, Francis Dyke Acland, Secretary to the Board of Agriculture, told farmers who were reluctant to employ women that 'if you won't, you are doing the Kaiser's work', and in the same month parliament received a statement that 'the danger point of greatly reduced production had already been reached'.[9] Such announcements explained the fervent rhetoric in the subsequent impassioned pleas for women and girls to apply to volunteer for farm work. One local newspaper article even claimed that 'the employment of women on the land would have a great effect on shortening the war'.[10] While a striking assertion, it was impossible to subsequently substantiate whether that was an accurate assessment.

There were also instances when irritation at women's hesitancy was expressed. One report bitterly complained that there were females 'perfectly able, and should be perfectly willing, to turn to help gather the products of the country, and save its people from starvation'.[11] One cause of reluctance was that wives of farm labourers serving in the war received a payment of 12/6d per week, plus, on a reducing scale, additional amounts for their children. That, understandably, resulted in a degree of diffidence to leave home environments for uncertain roles elsewhere. It was known, too, that women in other wartime occupations were paid more, and that 'farm work is hard and the town girl is liable to miss the joy of constant human intercourse'.[12]

The compelling need for additional female labour was made still more imperative when conscription of most medically fit unmarried men aged between 18 and 41 was imposed followed the passing of the Military

Services Act in January 1916. Just four months later a further raft of men, previously exempt, were called up. By February 1916, 250,000 men had left agricultural occupations and another 100,000 were expected to do so soon afterwards. That news led to an announcement that an increased number of 200,000 women and girls were required, but 'only 14,000 have so far come forward'.[13] The position was made even worse because in 1916 'crops had yielded badly',[14] a situation also apparent elsewhere in the world, notably in the large grain-producing areas of the United States of America and Canada.

If sufficient numbers of women were not persuaded to take up employment on farms, Rowland Prothero, who had succeeded Lord Selborne as President of the Board of Agriculture, estimated that 'the fall in numbers working on the land would have the effect of reducing the country's food production by fifteen to twenty-five per cent'.[15] As by mid-1917 the government believed that food stocks would last only three more weeks, Prothero warned that that prospect would be nothing short of a disaster.

# 3

# Hampshire's Responses to Labour Shortages on Farms up to 1916

In early 1915, elected members of Hampshire County Council approved the introduction of formal instruction of women and girls to meet a variety of farming needs. Indeed, it may have been the first county authority to do so. The Council's Sparsholt Farm School Special Sub-Committee noted in March 1915 that the government chose 'this school … where experiments might be made as to the efficiency and value of women's labour on farms'.[1] And five months later, Rowland Prothero, a Hampshire MP and later to be President of the Board of Agriculture, noted that the county was 'more favourable to the employment of women' and, particularly, provided 'longer training for women than in other parts of the country'.[2]

The senior Hampshire County Council officer who led the project to train women and girls for farm work was David Thomas Cowan, Hampshire's Director of Education. Born in Edinburgh, he trained as a science and art lecturer, taught at Beccles, and later became secretary to East Suffolk's Technical Education Committee. He moved to Hampshire in 1895 to become the county's Director of Technical Education and was promoted to the Director of Education post in 1903, a position he held until well beyond normal retirement age. Cowan devised the curriculum to provide four weeks of training, and it was said that to him 'belongs the credit of having formulated the scheme and for having, by patience and perseverance, brought it to the point of consummation'.[3] He retired in 1927 after a distinguished career spanning thirty-two years serving Hampshire's education services, and continued to live in Winchester until his death in 1936, aged 77.

Cowan had returned from the long-delayed government sponsored Agricultural Education Conference, and immediately tasked other council officials to encourage applications from girls who might be prepared to work on farms. In the meantime, he began planning the four-week training programme to be rolled out at Sparsholt's Farm School. Without central government guidance, he determined what aspects, relevant to Hampshire's farms, were to be taught, and how much effective instruction could be given in four weeks. To best serve the commonest range of local farming activities, the initial curriculum comprised caring for cattle, pigs and poultry, and the growing of horticultural products, notably, potatoes, cabbages and swedes. Cowan recognised that the various farming seasons would require different course programmes. In addition to outdoor farm-related teaching, recruits were to receive instruction in domestic duties, including the preparation of meals for staff, laundry work, and even mending socks. To maximise the chances of successful outcomes, and to achieve a low final drop-out rate, Cowan insisted that recruits made satisfactory progress in the first two weeks before being allowed to complete the instruction.

The Hampshire Farm School had moved its operations to Sparsholt barely a month after the war began. Although it had been realised in 1910 that Lower Mill Farm, Old Basing, had become too small to cater for the increasing demand for well-trained farm workers, two years elapsed considering many possible farm acquisitions before 251 acres of land and buildings at Westley Farm, on the outskirts of Sparsholt village, much nearer the county's centre, were purchased by Hampshire County Council[4] for £5,100. A further two years passed before the legal formalities were completed, new equipment was bought and installed, premises were adapted for training purposes, and the taxing transfer of existing animals and machinery took place. Most staff moved to Sparsholt, 25 miles from Old Basing, being persuaded to adjust their working and domestic lives to a different environment. Having done so, and after continuing for a short time to teach a wide variety of topics, mainly to boys, they were required to start instructing a different and narrower curriculum, almost entirely to girls and women, eight months later.

The initial group of twelve female students, aged between 17 and 30, began four weeks of training on Monday, 15 April 1915. Preparation for their arrival, towards the end of the Easter holiday period, had caused a two-week delay to the start of the scheduled summer term. That first course generated a great deal of public interest. Under the headings 'Women and Agricultural Work', 'Interesting Hampshire Experiment Reviewed', 'Partial Solution of a Difficult Problem', one of Hampshire's local newspapers produced a long and detailed article following completion of the initial training programme. An indication that Sparsholt may have been the first land-based institution to begin farming instruction also came from knowledge that just one of the twelve girls was a Hampshire resident. Others came from Bristol, Gloucester and Ross on Wye, while the remainder travelled from many different parts of the country. The newspaper's reporter concluded by commenting that, 'most of the girls have proved themselves wonderfully adaptable, and have cheerfully carried out their duties and shown themselves keen.'[5]

The first batch of Sparsholt's wartime female recruits, like those who came later, had to contend with long working days and little recreational time. The Farm School's principal, J. Duncan Davidson, decided to split the students into two groups, and after breakfast that began at 6.15 a.m., half undertook milking duties while the others made butter. Then, while some prepared the midday meal, others worked on a broad range of farm tasks: feeding calves and pigs; preparation of the ground for planting potatoes and cabbages; manure spreading; and 'couch burning' were examples. Lunch, then called 'dinner', was at 12.15 p.m., and in the afternoon, half were involved in domestic duties while the remainder had jobs on the farm or in the gardening section. After 'tea' and late afternoon milking, the trainees were able to play a piano provided for them in the common room or spend the evening on private study and their own interests – only until 9 p.m., though, when 'the bedtime bell is rung'.[6] They had just one half day off each week, on either Wednesday or Sunday afternoons, when leisure activities were permitted.

The social class profile of those attending Sparsholt's early four-week courses was widely reported. They were 'women of education – two were from a rectory' and were 'women of some culture',[7] and would, it was assumed, be quicker to learn and retain what was being taught. Another assessment was that they were 'well-educated and their social position is far above that of the ordinary labouring class'.[8]

That Hampshire view was echoed elsewhere; the Archdeacon of Exeter claimed that 'educated women would have little difficulty in adjusting to farm life',[9] but those from 'labouring classes' would struggle. However, by late 1916 it was found that women and girls from so-called 'labouring' households were equally adept at acquiring skills needed to work effectively on farms. After a more targeted advertisement programme, the economic background of students changed with a greater number of recruits coming from urban areas, especially London.

In the early years of the war, Sparsholt's students were charged 'a fee of 10/- per week to include tuition, board and lodging',[10] later raised to 12/6d. Fees were, however, abandoned in 1917 when urgency to remove inhibiting factors constraining the increase in the number of recruits was needed. Before that decision was made nationally, Hampshire's War Agricultural Executive Committee ('War Ag')[11] had agreed to waive fees for some candidates, including three local girls who showed promise but for whom the cost would have been too great a burden on family incomes. Over the remainder of 1915, Sparsholt successfully trained eighty women for farm work, sixty of whom stayed in Hampshire to be employed on local farms.

'English girls learning the trade of farming to take the place of farmers who have gone off to war, Sparsholt, Hampshire, England, 26 April 1915. Here they are seen following the harrow.' (Getty Images, serial no. 167182537; Underwood Archives)

Westley Farmhouse, Sparsholt, built circa 1870. (Sparsholt College)

For Cowan's plans to be effectively implemented, competent and dedicated staff were essential. People capable of caring for dairy herds were in particularly short supply, and the Farm School was fortunate to have attracted Mary Darrell, a highly regarded expert. Born into a Yorkshire farming family, she had worked at University College of Wales, Aberystwyth, as 'senior dairy instructress' since about 1895. When Darrell moved to Hampshire in 1901, her principal greatly regretted her departure, and expressed his 'highest testimony to her ability and character'.[12] She served Hampshire's education authority with immense commitment before, during and after the war, returning to Yorkshire in 1920 to farm in partnership with her sister.

Training in domestic duties, including laundry work and meal preparation, was under the direction of Margaret Broadbent. She came to Sparsholt, just as the war began, from teaching posts in Cheshire, being described as 'cookery teacher' in the 1911 population census. Broadbent taught students at Sparsholt and Hampshire schools for twenty-five years until she retired in 1939. She came to national prominence in the 1930s as a leading member of the National Union of Women Teachers, formed in 1920 following a split from the

National Union of Teachers to campaign more fervently for better terms and conditions for women teachers.

An even longer serving member of staff was Charles J. Gleed. He took charge of horticultural instruction at Old Basing in 1911 and was active in encouraging gardening groups around the county at the time when increased production was badly needed. He was a respected expert, leading the trialling of varieties of potato and the effect of different manures and soils on yields and profitability. In late 1916, Gleed was appointed 'acting' principal after Davidson, his predecessor, departed suddenly after conviction for gross cruelty to a Farm School horse, for which he was fined £25, the equivalent of approximately £2,700 in 2024. Gleed undertook the role for four years, overseeing the training of women and girl recruits in addition to his normal duties. He retired in 1948 after thirty-seven years at Sparsholt and Old Basing, and died in Winchester in 1971, aged 88.

The appeals for women to replace large numbers of male agricultural workers, and to maintain and increase the acreage under cultivation, became more and more intensive. While the vital role that women and girls played during the war eventually became widely acknowledged, the roles undertaken by farm training institutions, not least Sparsholt, needs more recognition. Over and above their instruction to residential recruits, staff visited many Hampshire voluntary groups to share their expertise, encourage the home growing of produce, and to judge gardening and horticultural competitions. In addition to Sparsholt, there were other residential training institutions, notably: Seale Hayne Agricultural College at Newton Abbot, South Devon; Harper Adams Agricultural College, at Egmond, near Newport, Shropshire; Monmouthshire Institute of Agriculture at Usk; and Swanley Horticultural College, Kent, then providing training for women only. Some wealthy landowners, mainly located in south-east English counties, offered their farms for teaching purposes, but many were disadvantaged in not being able to provide sufficient living accommodation.

In the early years of the war, despite an assertion that 'women were capable of doing many jobs on the farm very well',[13] a minority of farmers were 'unwilling to avail themselves of the services of women. Much of this reflected the farmers' prejudices and conservatism…'[14] Certainly, the prospect of females working on Hampshire's farms was not universally accepted. The reluctance of some farmers was designed, in part, to persuade the authorities to allow their male employees to remain on farms and not have to leave to join the armed forces. Among other grumbles, a Hampshire fruit grower 'once had a woman from college who caused him more trouble in a fortnight than he had in a year', and in the same paper another farmer was said to have 'tried the experiment [to employ women] but the women had thrown up the job. He would rather give up his land than employ female labour.'[15] In January 1916, the *Hampshire Independent* reported that 'the reluctance of farmers to employ women was very much less than it was three months ago',[16] but that claim seemed overly optimistic given that a few farmers continued voicing strident reservations. Sometimes it was doubted that 'women were physically and constitutionally strong enough to take the place of men', while others claimed that 'women were weak or squeamish, or ill-disciplined, or empty headed'.[17] The perceived resistance of girls to accept legitimate authority was encapsulated in a comment from a farmer who 'had great difficulty with their discipline. It was no use for the women to run off home when a shower of rain came.'[18]

From a quite different perspective, Mary Darrell, the Sparsholt staff member who regularly toured Hampshire as part of her dairy teaching duties, was moved to write in October 1916:

> It amazes me to notice how few women are employed in this occupation, in spite of the war, the scarcity of men, and all that people like myself, who have devoted their lives to the work, have said on the subject. One can still go through village after village and not see a single woman milker! For this deplorable state of affairs our farmers must be blamed. They will not employ women so long as they can obtain men.[19]

Because objections from farmers regularly appeared, War Work for Women committees were established in all English counties to try and minimise adverse comments. Hampshire's committee was established in April 1915, well within the deadline of August 1915 set by Lord Selborne for all counties to comply with his instruction. Florence Anita Eyre Baring, Countess of Northbrook, was appointed 'chairman', serving at the same time that her husband, the Earl of Northbrook, was chairman of the 'War Ag' committee. For her wartime service, she was appointed to the Red Cross Honours List in 1918 and was awarded a CBE in 1920.

To enlarge the potential supply of girls, unsuccessful attempts were made to reduce the minimum age of recruitment to 14. By early 1916, the need for women farm workers in Hampshire had become acute. At a War Work for Women Committee meeting in Fareham, Miss Cooper, of the Board of Agriculture, said that there was a 'want of labour to keep up home-grown food supply'. It was essential to employ 'women on the land in those lighter branches of work'[20] to replace the 200,000 men who had by then left the land to fight. That number increased substantially to around 350,000 by the end of 1916. Hampshire's committee was, though, later pleased to report that 400 women were employed on the county's farms, and by June 1916 '2,378 women have registered for work on the land in Hampshire'.[21] Nationally, the number had grown to 35,000, more than double the 16,000 women working on farms in December 1915.

There were many issues for the Countess of Northbrook and other committee members to address. The selection and training of sufficient numbers of girls and women, the allocation of placements to farms, the sourcing of residential accommodation, the management of income from government and scrutiny of expenditure, supervision and care for the increasing number of women and girls on farms, and the selection and monitoring of farmers to train those who could not get, or want, a place at Sparsholt, were examples of the matters to be dealt with.

One of the national issues with local implications was the level of wages paid to women working on farms. Existing wage rates for women already employed in 1915 were usually 1/- per day, with 1/6d sometimes paid to the woman who arrived first! Based on his examination of job advertisements in local newspapers, a Hampshire county councillor with extensive farming interests was concerned that those who succeeded in passing the Sparsholt course would be seeking 'prohibitive wages of 30/- or 35/- a week. That, he said, was totally unaffordable.'[22] His view was not borne out by future experience. In November 1916, between eighty-five and a hundred trained women already working on Isle of Wight farms were being paid 15/- per week, a far cry from the £3 or £4 apparently paid to those working in munition factories, and less than a half the amount feared by the county councillor. The same subject was considered by the Romsey and District branch of Hampshire's 'War Ag' committee in March 1916, when it agreed that 'three pence per hour [was] to be paid to each woman for ordinary work, and three [and a] half-penny for harvesting and haymaking'.[23]

Demonstrating the importance of the War Work for Women Committee responsibilities, the Countess of Northbrook was supported by other influential Hampshire women. Laura Joan Chute, whose husband was a leading Hampshire county councillor, was appointed to chair the committee's hotel branch. That group had the demanding and time-consuming task of acquiring suitable accommodation. It sought private homes, existing buildings for adaptation, and farmhouses, all as billets, as well as hostels large enough for significant numbers of residents. Those women and girls living in properties occupied by farmers had mixed experiences; some were wholehearted welcomed and became part of the families, while others much preferred living in hostels with other land workers.

Mary Katherine Cook, who was the county's organising secretary throughout the First World War, undertook the challenging executive operational responsibilities. Known as 'Kitty', she was born in 1887, the daughter of a senior master at Winchester College and his wife. On one occasion, Cook reported that, 'on the whole the Sparsholt girls have done exceedingly well,' although she went on to say that of sixty-one trainees who attended in a part of one year 'nine were turned down as useless'.[24] At the end of the war, she was thanked for 'how hard she worked for the woman land-worker, and she has taken care to help them in every way possible'.[25] Among other accomplishments, Cook exercised musical talent as a well-regarded cello player, a leading Women's Institute choir member and, in the 1930s, as orchestral secretary to the Winchester and County Music Festival. She moved to London in 1940 and, unusually for a woman at that time, was elected mayor of Chelsea in 1952 and 1953. Her character might be judged by a comment made after her death in 1960 that leaves little to the imagination: 'a generous frame and a booming voice, she expressed firmly held views quite forcefully'.[26]

A member of another well-known Hampshire family played an important part in the work of the committee. A Miss Freshfield, one of five unmarried daughters of Rev. John Freshfield, rector of Easton, and his wife, took the leading role in interviewing and selecting candidates to undertake farm work. While it is not certain which of the five daughters served the committee, it is likely to have been Jessie Freshfield, who was later created a Dame of the Order of St John. One of Jessie's sisters, Agnes Cecilia, served on the county committee that was, effectively, the governing body of Sparsholt's Farm School.

By far the youngest committee member was Pauline Woolmer White, who was born in 1891. In January 1918 she received a certificate signed by Arthur Lee, Director General of Food Production, and Rowland E. Prothero, President of the Board of Agriculture, expressing thanks for her contribution in maximising the involvement of women in her capacity as supervisor to Hampshire's 'War Ag' committee. The wording stated that, 'Every woman who helps in agriculture during the war is as truly serving her country as the man who is fighting in the trenches, on the sea, or in the air.'[27] Like many young women who suffered the same war-years experience, her boyfriend was killed while serving abroad in the armed forces,[28] and this might have given added impetus to her future extensive commitment. A member of the family that founded the firm of Timothy White which developed into a chain of chemist shops, sold to Boots Pure Drug Ltd in 1968, Pauline Woolmer White retained her advocacy of Hampshire's WLA for very many years as she had senior involvement throughout the Second World War, and beyond.

In addition to Hampshire's central committee, local bodies were quickly set up. Supportive residents at Petersfield produced a report within a week of an initial meeting in July 1915, giving a list of farming tasks they believed women could undertake:

> (1) more or less unskilled temporary farm work, such as picking hops or hoeing turnips or putting sheaves into shucks; (2) skilled farm work; (3) market gardening; (4) working in private gardens; (5) working on land specially lent.[29]

As part of a campaign to encourage many women and girls to volunteer, two Petersfield committee members made themselves available each week to talk individually with interested people. In parallel with that work, farmers were asked to be prepared to take on women employees.

By April 1916, nineteen of the county's twenty-two districts were actively canvassing for recruits. At Waterlooville at the end of a well-attended meeting 'no fewer than 40 ladies gave in their names for whole-time or part-time work',[30] and at about the same time a meeting at Purbrook, a village on the outskirts of Waterlooville, also had a successful outcome. The same pattern of local groups in Hampshire was followed in most English counties, and by February 1916, twenty-five had established committees, all designed to try and attract potential female farm workers.

The widening scope of jobs to be performed by women and girls was exemplified by another need in which Hampshire had a direct and important involvement. The British army requisitioned a huge number of horses and mules as it had 'an insatiable demand for horses to haul guns, transport munitions and even go into battle'.[31] As part of the process to get the horses ready, the Board of Agriculture established three strategically placed, large Horse Remount Depots around the country. The first was at Pauncefoot Farm, on the Broadlands Estate, Romsey, where preparatory building work began in November 1914, with the first animals arriving in March 1915.[32] The vast facility covered nearly 500 acres, grew rapidly, and accommodated 2,000 people and up to 5,000 animals by the end of 1916. While many horses came from England and Ireland, large numbers were also shipped from America to Devonport, near Plymouth, and brought from South Devon to Romsey by train.

By 1917, the Romsey Depot had received, health checked and trained an estimated 368,000 horses for transfer to France. In just three days in March 1917, 1,200 horses were walked from the Romsey Depot to the port at Southampton, a distance of 9 or 10 miles. Close by, at North Stoneham, a Swaythling Remount Depot was another focal point for the despatch of large numbers of animals from Southampton. With the constant need to keep adding to the numbers of men serving abroad with the armed forces, women steadily replaced men at the Romsey Depot to care for and train the horses and mules. After the war, those animals that had survived the conflict were returned to England, and in April 1919, 757 people were still at the Swaythling Depot caring for 3,500 horses. The facilities at Romsey and Swaythling were closed down in 1920,[33] and in February that year 480 huts and sixty-eight horse shelters at the Romsey Depot were advertised for sale.

Romsey Remount Depot, Isolation Hospital. (National archive catalogue no. WO161/117)

Memorial Statue in Romsey War Memorial Park, commemorating the work of the Romsey Remount Depot.

Some owners did not wish to have their horses requisitioned and went to great lengths to keep them. Thomas Heslop Hill had moved from Chettle House, near Blandford, Dorset, to the extensive Redenham Estate, Weyhill, near Andover, at around the start of the war. Although then in his mid-60s, he was still a keen huntsman and, in advance of a visit to purloin his horses in early 1915, he moved two animals from the estate's fields, hid them in one of several cellars located around the estate's buildings, and succeeded in 'hood winking' the authorities.[34] Hill died soon afterwards at the Royal Palace Hotel, Kensington, London, in October 1915, leaving an estate valued at £86,442. He was first interred in the estate grounds but was later buried in the nearby churchyard of the parish church of St Peter and St Paul, Thruxton.

Women had two roles in connection with this massive operation. While an increasing number of women took over from men at Romsey, the workforce at a depot set up later in Wiltshire was made up entirely of women. And secondly, because of the colossal loss of horses on farms, it was crucial that women were taught to drive tractors and to use other mechanical implements that were beginning to be delivered to British farms in considerable quantities. From fewer than 1,000 tractors when the war began, there were 6,000 on farms by 1918.

Despite the success of county bodies in training and recruiting women and girls for service on farms, those vital responsibilities were removed from local authority control in August 1917, and taken over by the Women's Section of the Food Production Department of the Board of Agriculture. Fortunately, although the potential food crisis became ever more obvious and serious, there continued to be no shortage of Hampshire residents prepared to do all they could to attract land-based workers. Some farmers still had reservations that they expressed in forceful and colourful language, but they were greatly outnumbered by those who quickly saw the urgency of finding a solution to the problem, and recognised the value that women brought to the tasks.

# 4

# The Women's Land Army from March 1917, Nationally and in Hampshire[1]

William Palmer, 2nd Earl of Selborne, appointed President of the Board of Agriculture in May 1915, had many links with Hampshire, his family's home being Blackmoor House, Selborne. Before having government ministerial responsibility given to him, he had been elected Liberal MP for Petersfield in 1885 and again in 1892. He later became warden of Winchester College from 1920 to 1925, and was high steward of Winchester from 1929 until his death in 1942. He had the mandate to maximise the supply of home-grown food produce. A clear enough aim but, recognising the huge and growing shortfall in replacing male agricultural labourers, and the long-term declining trend in the numbers of women working on farms, a fundamental cultural shift was required. In addition to the need to replace men, it was necessary to reduce food shortage risks associated with imports by sea by requiring more home-grown produce. Palmer instigated the establishment of county 'War Ag' committees that comprised influential figures, giving status and authority to those charged with overcoming the challenges ahead. His vision, though, was soon frustrated and, prompted by disagreement with the coalition government's policy about Home Rule for Ireland, he resigned in July 1916.

Selborne was succeeded by Rowland E. Prothero, who also had Hampshire connections. His father was an Isle of Wight clergyman, and Rowland had played cricket for Hampshire between 1875 and 1883.

In his government role, he instigated and anticipated the imminent formation of the WLA. Addressing farmers in Newport, Monmouthshire, in January 1917, he told his audience that the 'women will be paid soldiers' pay and billeted like soldiers and uniformed like soldiers'.[2] By then, 100 women were already working on Isle of Wight farms, and several hundred more were employed on Hampshire's mainland. To address ongoing labour shortages, the possibility of using German and Italian prisoners of war was examined, as well as the encouragement of school-children to assist with harvesting in holiday times.[3]

William Palmer, 2nd Earl Selborne, President, Board of Agriculture, 1915–1916. (Bassano Ltd, via Wikipedia)

Prothero had earlier established a Women's Section of the National Services Department which, in March 1917, became the WLA as a branch of the Food Production Department. He envisaged a properly organised national campaign with clear objectives 'to procure, train and equip a large number of female workers able and willing to devote their whole time to agricultural work wherever they are required'.[4] Part-time work was not to be allowed, a minimum age of 18 was imposed, and applicants were expected to be in good general health.

The government's formal establishment of the WLA in March 1917 provided the necessary impetus to increase the number of female land workers. It had taken the Board of Agriculture two and a half years from the start of the First World War in August 1914 to debate, plan and set up the organisation that coordinated the valiant efforts already being made by other groups. Considerable numbers of women who had already been supporting farming activities in these bodies gave the WLA a promising start.

The first key appointment was that of Meriel Talbot as the WLA's director. She had previously been the Board of Agriculture's first woman inspector, so she would have known the extent of the huge challenge facing her. Despite plenty of ups and downs along the way, she eventually oversaw the recruitment of over 23,000 women and girls who, by huge efforts, enabled food production to be maintained, and later increased, to meet the nation's needs. Talbot served as the WLA's director until it was disbanded in 1919, when she became a government adviser on women's employment matters. For her distinguished public service, she was awarded an OBE in 1917, and was appointed a Dame Commander of the Order of the British Empire (CBE) in 1920.

The need for more women and girls to come forward was urgent and appeals for 'a rush of patriotic women'[5] aged 18 years and over were passionately made. In April 1917, Prothero told an audience that women 'must be of good constitution and vigorous', and called for 'milkers, plough women, carters, field workers, cow women, market gardeners',[6] all to be paid a minimum wage of 18/- per week. Five thousand were required for milking and dairying jobs, and the same number for general farm work. Ships bringing imports to Britain were regularly being sunk by enemy ships and U-boats, those from Norway bringing timber being especially vulnerable. The resultant shortages were so significant that Prothero called for additional volunteers to fell trees, with the timber used to provide pit props, railway sleepers and army huts.

An early 1917 leaflet addressed to 'Women War Land Workers' noted that recruits 'will be called a War Land Worker', given the prospect of 'promotion to Group Leader', and the possibility of further promotion to 'Instructor in a Training Centre'. Even at the earliest stage of WLA's existence, the possibility was floated that:

> selected members of the Women's Land Army who wish, after the war, to farm on their own account and to form themselves into groups for this purpose, will be separately registered, and every effort will be made to secure for them special facilities for settlement on the land, either at home or in the Dominions overseas.[7]

However, perversely, initial attempts to recruit additional workers for land-based jobs were directed at men, not women. A 1917 National

Service 'Waistcoat pocket note for Speakers' was prepared to encourage recruitment into many occupations, including agriculture, but that section referred to 'every man between the ages of eighteen and sixty-one'. Furthermore, a letter from the National Services Department in March 1917 noted the 'urgent necessity for every man with a knowledge of ploughing being placed at the disposal of agriculture during the next two months'.[8] As the requirement for men to be deployed in the armed forces grew, it became obvious that a shift in advertising focus was necessary to encourage many more women and girls to apply for farm work. An undated leaflet, probably issued in the summer of 1917, changed the underlying message by stressing that 'male substitutes should not be provided for any work which can be done by women'.[9]

Advertisements for women agricultural workers appeared with eye-catching exhortations. Huge A3-size posters with strap lines 'God Speed the Plough and the Women who Drive it' and 'Don't Delay – Enrol Today' were two. The posters urged women to obtain application forms from post offices or employment exchanges. While some posters had a few words in bold lettering and colours, others went into more detail, one saying that girls and women could expect suitable clothing, travelling expenses and 18/- per week or the 'district' rate if that was higher. They were assured that accommodation to be provided would be 'personally inspected and approved'[10] by a 'War Ag' committee member in each county.

While the initial 1917 aim was to attract another 10,000 women and girls, within a few months a further impetus was required. The first applicants were encouraged from the more educated families, but a July 1917 letter acknowledged that 'girls of the industrial class' could be suitable, as could those 'living in suburbs of large towns'.[11] There was, though, a note of caution in one leaflet which, while stressing the 'pressing and vital necessity' for more recruits, warned that 'considerable wastage takes place with enrolments from ineligible and unsuitable volunteers'.[12] This created an obvious dilemma. Ever more women and girls were needed to replace men, but strict criteria were to be applied as 'applicants were rigorously questioned about their health, physical capabilities and reasons for wishing to become a land worker'.[13] Priority was given to those who had some farming experience and to those not in work, but there were other requirements: only in exceptional

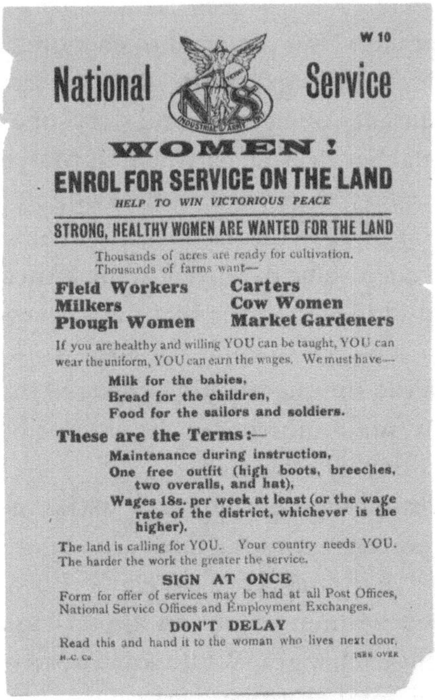

'WOMEN Wanted at Once FOR THE LAND'.

'The Women's Land Army needs YOU to-day'.

circumstances were girls under the age of 20 to be employed, and an assessment was made of a candidate's temperament to ensure that those selected could cope with all that farm working entailed. Furthermore, they had to agree to work anywhere in the country and, having been provisionally accepted for the WLA, recruits were told whether formal training at a land-based institution was needed, or whether they would start work on a farm immediately.

To address the local need for volunteers, Winchester City Council members promptly set about establishing a committee consisting of city councillors and prominent business leaders. The first meeting was held at Abbey House on 9 February 1917, with the minutes referring to a 'Private and informal meeting of the Town Council of the City of Winchester'. One outcome was a decision to invite a government-selected person to speak at a public meeting designed to attract recruits to enrol for one of the many options available. The MP chosen to visit Winchester on 22 February 1917 was Arthur Shirley Benn, Conservative MP for Plymouth, and a member of the government's Ammunition Committee. He was advised to catch the 4 p.m. train from Waterloo that was due to arrive at Winchester at 6.15 p.m. – a far cry from the sixty-one minutes of the fastest trains today!

As the war progressed, another issue made the need to recruit women and girls even more urgent. In addition to the replacement of huge numbers of men going abroad to fight, there was a pressing requirement, not just to maintain production, but to substantially increase acreage under cultivation. The government's target was to add another 2.5 million acres between January 1917 and the end of 1918, and each county's 'War Ag' committee was given responsibility for achieving its share. The government was eventually pleased with the progress made, recording that by the summer of 1917 the acreage of wheat was the highest since 1882, barley and oats had increased by 20 per cent, and potatoes by 27 per cent compared with the previous year.[14] Nonetheless, an article in *The Times* in November 1917 drew the government's attention 'to the dangers of the food queues which are rapidly "arriving"'.[15]

The need for the substantially increased home production recognised that in 1914, 60 per cent of British food came from abroad. After just a short time, however, imports of cereals, sugar and dairy products had reduced drastically, partly caused by the devastating effect of German

U-boat activity. In the four months from October 1916 to January 1917, 1.4 million tonnes of merchant shipping were sunk. Quite apart from the huge loss of essential food supplies, there was a large number of civilian deaths. A year later, David Lloyd George, then prime minister, in one of his famous speeches, asserted that 'the German submarines are trying to starve us by sinking the ships which are used to carry to our shores the abundant harvests of other lands'.[16] During the four years of the war, it was estimated that German U-boats sank almost 5,000 ships comprising nearly 13 million gross registered tonnage, 6 million tonnes in 1917 alone.[17] Inevitably, with demand far exceeding supply, food prices rose substantially, by 42 per cent in 1916.

By the middle of 1917, there were 247 training centres throughout the country, as well as 140 'practice farms', providing capacity to train large numbers of recruits. In addition to the Farm School at Sparsholt, there were at least three other Hampshire centres giving instruction. One was the Hill House Training Centre, Sherborne St John, near Basingstoke, where Woolmer White was supervisor for a while. She passed her responsibility to Miss Churcher who, in 1919, was said to have provided 'a splendid example to the girls under her, giving encouragement and advice to those about to leave the Institute for their various farms'.[18] Another property in the northern part of the county that became a training centre was Lyde Green Farmhouse, Rotherwick, near Hook. Here, Frederick James Smith entered into a tenancy agreement with authorised officials of the WLA to make the farmhouse available as a 'Training Centre and Home for Women's Land Army Land Workers' at a rent of £1 per week.[19]

On the Isle of Wight, Veniscombe House, Newchurch, now a Grade 2 listed property built in about 1830, became a hostel and training centre in early 1917. Gertrude Perrott, a wealthy Ryde, Isle of Wight, resident, and an active supporter of the WLA, offered the house rent free. It could accommodate up to nine women and girls, and came with a paddock and 1 acre of garden. A letter to a local newspaper told readers of the owner's generosity and stressed the need for a constant supply of recruits to come forward to benefit from four weeks' instruction in gardening and poultry keeping.[20] A newspaper report in April 1917 stated that the first batch of trained students were ready to be placed on local farms, and suggested that Veniscombe House was, other than well-established land-based institutions, 'the first opened under the National Service and Board of Agriculture Scheme'.[21] If so, Hampshire's claim to be in the forefront of WLA recruitment and training was further confirmed. Perrott was also an active member of Isle of Wight branches of several national organisations, including the War Pensions Committee, and President of the Soldiers and Sailors Families Association.[22] A Justice of the Peace for many years, she died in 1964, aged 96.

The numbers of full-time WLA employees on farms grew modestly from 6,000 in September 1917 to 7,000 by April 1918, but after a particularly successful campaign, to 16,000 in September 1918. That rise was helped by a decision in early 1918 that a commitment of six months rather than a year would be acceptable. Notwithstanding that relaxation, the demanding selection process resulted in only 25 per cent of volunteers in some parts of the country being accepted as WLA recruits. Despite the increasing number of women employed on British farms, more resource was needed, and an appeal went out for men to help with the 1917 harvest. Ten thousand were said to be required to bring in the hay, and 15,000 to garner the grain harvest a few months later. To supplement the employment of women and girls, a Junior Land Army was contemplated that would comprise boys and girls under 18 years of age to assist with market gardening and other relatively light farm work.

Women's Land Army Rally, Andover, 1916. (WLA website)

Imaginative ways were used to attract recruits for farms. One such was in Portsmouth, when two senior national members of the WLA touring the country spoke in a local theatre following a performing dog act. They apparently received a good, though boisterous, reception from an audience largely made up of sailors on leave from their own war service.[23] Appeals were also made on cinema screens and from church pulpits.

Recruiting enough people for farms remained a challenge, despite the value of farm work undertaken by WLA members becoming more generally recognised. Thomas Christian, a man of great influence in Hampshire's agricultural circles, told a recruitment rally at Portsmouth in June 1918 that he had been a farmer for fifty years, had employed many women and girls, 'and could most thoroughly testify to their efficiency'.[24] Among his non-farming activities, Christian became vice chairman of Droxford Rural District Council, was a life-long total abstainer, and a well-respected Wesleyan Methodist local preacher. He was a leading advocate of the short-lived Independent Agricultural Parliamentary Party, established in 1907 because it was felt that the two dominant political parties failed to sufficiently address farming issues. Little progress was made and although it was reconstituted as the Rural Party in 1923, with the intention of fielding general election candidates in seventy English constituencies, the change failed to bring success and the party was dissolved in 1924. At Christian's funeral in 1929 it was said that his commitment to the cause had made him a suitable person to be the party's leader,[25] although that event did not happen.

Despite frequent references to the prospect of impending food shortages, rationing was delayed until 1918. This may have been because WLA members had contributed to successes in minimising the impact of reduced imports by the increase in home production. Rationing was foretold in January when David A. Thomas, Viscount Rhondda, in his capacity as Minister of Food Control, spoke to a gathering at the Mansion House, London, telling his audience that 'we are faced with a grave situation … I regard compulsory rationing as inevitable and urgent.'[26] A few days later, in January 1918, sugar was rationed with meat, butter, margarine and cheese following in April, and lard in July. Every resident was issued with a ration book and had to register with a local grocer. Prices of key products were set by government decree and reviewed regularly. When the scheme was fully operational, each person was, as examples, entitled to '10d worth of "butcher's meat", 4 ounces of butter and margarine, 1½ ounces of lard and 8 ounces of sugar'.[27]

In Hampshire, the need to issue ration books urgently resulted in drastic steps being taken. Southampton's Food Control Committee employed up to 250 schoolteachers for evening work, paying them 1/- per hour. They processed 25,000 applications in three months, although over 10,000 had to be returned for additions or corrections to be made.[28] In February 1918, Winchester City Council closed every school for half a day so that teachers could deal with 40,000 applications.[29] The easing of rationing began in 1920. In March, the sugar ration was increased from 6 ounces to 8 ounces, the butter ration was increased, and the restriction on potatoes ended altogether. A year later, in March 1921, bacon and butter were the last two items to have rationing removed.

Perhaps because Sparsholt's Farm School had already been training women and girls for two years, an announcement in March 1917 of 'four weeks free training (including board and lodging) ... is offered to suitable women willing to train for work on the land'[30] was a low-key advertisement in local newspapers. In the last full year of the war to September 1918, 120 recruits had successfully passed through the Farm School, suggesting that the total number of women and girls trained at Sparsholt since 1915 was between 400 and 500. That clearly demonstrated that its capacity to meet Hampshire's demand was insufficient, resulting in many women, perhaps four or five times that number, being taught at other training centres and on approved farms. In addition, some specialist teaching, thatching being an example, was not offered at Sparsholt and had to be undertaken elsewhere.

By the end of the war, the 23,000 full-time members of the WLA had been divided into three branches, with the original 'Agricultural' section having over 12,000 members. In the autumn of 1918, a statistical breakdown was made of the occupations of women on farms. Given that many would have been engaged in more than one activity, caution is needed in assessing the full validity of the results. It was claimed that 5,734 were 'Milkers' and another 3,971 employed as 'Field Workers', together making up two-thirds of the total number. Of the remainder, 635 were 'carters', 515 worked in 'Market gardens', 260 in 'Private Gardens', 260 were 'Ploughwomen', and 293 were 'Tractor drivers'. The balance was spread between 'Forewomen', 'Threshers', 'Thatchers', 'Shepherds' and 'Bailiffs'. The final category, 'Other branches', numbered 653, making a grand total of 12,639.[31]

Much less publicity was given to the work undertaken by the 'Foraging' and 'Forestry' sections of the WLA. The Women's Forage Corps was established by the government in 1915 when the army became heavily dependent on horses. By 1917, over 600,000 animals had been provided to the British army for cavalry operations, leading to the need for many people to provide food and care for them. The work also involved 'the packing and loading of bales, and chaff-cutting'[32] as part of ensuring the well-being of the animals, assistance with haymaking, the making and repairing of sacks, and the distribution of hay to front lines. As the Forage Corps was closely connected to the army, members were normally based in army camps and depots. There was an active group based at Romsey,[33] but one local comment noted that, 'the Forage Corps is a branch of the women's service that is not so well known as its plucky girls deserve to be.'[34] Long hours and hard physical work were evident, with pay claimed to be equal to that of soldiers. The Forage Corps became part of the WLA in 1917 with a membership that peaked at 8,000. It continued as a separate organisation for a few months after the formal demobilisation of the WLA in November 1919, by which time its membership was still 6,000.

Also set up as a distinct body in 1916 was the Women's Forestry Corps, having two defined groups, both requiring much physical strength. One was involved in tree felling and the other with the measuring and sawing up of timber into the required sizes for a multitude of uses, notably paper production, building ships, huts for the accommodation of soldiers and for the railways. Again, little publicity was given to the strenuous work of the Forestry Corps. One local newspaper comment was that 'during the last two years [from 1916] a patriotic group of young women have been planting trees'[35] in the New Forest. The Women's Forestry Corps, which, by the end of the war, had 4,000 members, had also been integrated into the WLA in 1917.

There was no shortage of accolades for WLA members as the war drew to a close and victory celebrations were anticipated. A November 1918 article in the *Hampshire Advertiser* was especially appreciative. A.T. Matthews, a regular feature writer on agricultural matters, had some perceptive messages to impart. He had been a firm advocate of the WLA, and in an article headed 'Women's Land Labour' he was fulsome in his praise:

> The war has had an immense effect on the status of women in the world of business, and they have now attained such a position in that of politics that those who expect the sex to fall back into the old ruts of the days of peace are surely reckoning without their host.

He later added that 'to push the sex on one side now that the great crisis is past would, indeed, be the height of ingratitude', and 'our women literally came to the rescue of the nation, and had they not done so, it is little less than appalling to think of the dire straits we should have been in'. Decades before his time, Matthews also called for 'equal pay for equal work'.[36]

Six months before the war ended, a meeting took place in the council chamber of Winchester Rural District Council on 14 May 1918 that suggested a developing link between the WLA and the Women's Institute in Hampshire. On that date, the Hampshire Federation of Women's Institutes, then consisting of about fifteen groups, was established at a meeting chaired by the Countess of Northbrook, who had been intimately involved in the county's WLA since 1915. In attendance was Gertrude Mary Denman, Lady Denman.[37] She was later appointed Honorary Director of the WLA in 1939 at the start of the Second World War in addition to her 'Chairmanship' of the National Federation of Women's Institutes that began in 1916. As was certainly the case after the WLA was finally demobilised in November 1950, Women's Institute branches may well, from 1918 onwards, have provided support to women and girls who needed it when they gave up their employment with Hampshire's farmers and had to adjust to a quite different life.

Acknowledgement of the positive contributions made by women came in different forms. Certificates were issued to those leaving the WLA with the wording encouraging more recruits to come forward: 'Every woman who helps in agriculture during the war is as truly serving her country as the man who is fighting in the trenches, on the sea, or in the air.' As a modicum of further recognition for the immense contributions made by Hampshire's WLA members, after completion of 240 hours of work, probably equating to five or six weeks' full-time

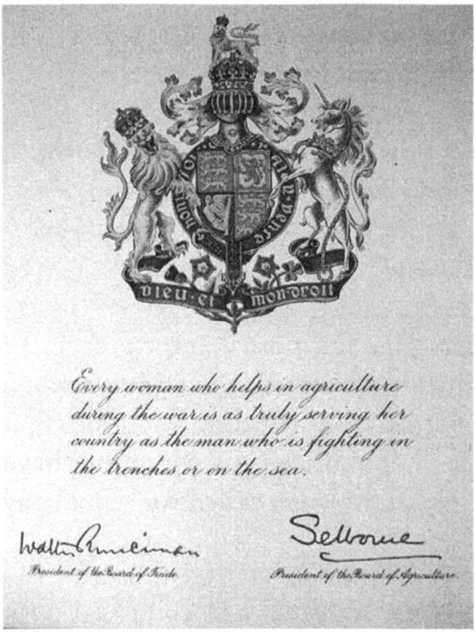


Certificate signed by Rowland Prothero and Arthur Lee.

Good Service Ribbon Badge (Land Army Agricultural Section).

employment, arm bands and official badges were issued. Members whose work was especially appreciated received a 'Good Service Ribbon' badge, awarded to those who had served continuously for six months and 'kept up a high standard of work and conduct'.[38]

One expression of gratitude, early in 1918, reporting on a rally attended by 230 WLA members in Winchester, referred to the girls looking 'healthy and happy … and their smart appearance did them much credit' and they were 'workmanlike and dapper in appearance'. There were, though, occasional notes of caution for WLA members. The handbook issued to every member of the Agricultural section reminded them that:

> you are doing a man's work and so you are dressed rather like a man, but remember just because you wear a smock and breeches you should take care to behave like a British girl who expects chivalry and respect from everyone she meets.[39]

Dame Edith Lyttleton, Deputy Director of the Women's Branch of the Board of Agriculture, during a speech in 1918, referred to a 'minor drawback' of complaints about the uniform issued to WLA members but said that women and girls should 'stick it out to the end'.[40] Complaints about the unsuitability of WLA uniform also emerged from land girls in the Second World War. Lyttleton held two other senior positions associated with advancing the interests of women: the executive of the National Union of Women Workers and, between 1916 and 1925, the Central Committee of Women's Employment.

While it was the case throughout the war that members of the WLA were paid less than their counterparts in other wartime occupations, wage rates of a minimum of 18/- per week in 1917 had risen during the following two years, to 20/- per week in March 1918, and to 25/- in April 1919, subject to training being successfully completed. The valuable role of women was not, however, measured by monetary considerations. Rather, success in maintaining and then increasing food production to minimise the loss of imports, was, and remains, a more appropriate way of judging their contributions to the overall war effort.

# 5

# Post-war Experience

Many testimonies to the work of WLA members were published in December 1918, immediately after the war ended, and well into 1919. At government level, Lord Lee of Fareham, President of the Board of Agriculture, expressed his appreciation in a long letter published in the December 1918 edition of *The Landswoman*:

> The Women's Land Army is entitled to a specially honourable place among the various bodies into which women were organised. In spite of lower wages than might have been obtained in other occupations and in spite of the isolation and discomforts of farm life, they came forward in large numbers to take the places of men who had to leave the land for the army. In almost every kind of farm work they have proved themselves most efficient substitutes for men and it is certain that the greatly increased production which was secured from the land during the war could not have been achieved without the Women's Land Army. I cannot omit a special tribute to the cheerfulness of spirit of comradeship which have been such conspicuous features.[1]

Another letter of appreciation came from Rowland Prothero, the previous minister responsible for agriculture: 'Their [WLA members] sacrifice is made without the spur of winning glory'. Rev. Frederick B. Meyer, a leading Baptist minister known as 'the Archbishop of the Free Churches', thanked members for 'the splendid manner in which you have stepped into the breach and solved the problems of maintaining British Agriculture'.[2] Lord Lee later noted that, 'all ranks of the Land Army can look back with pride to their share in developing home production of food during the war, and they may be assured that their self-sacrifice service will never be forgotten.'[3] By the end of the war, there was an overwhelming sense of gratitude to WLA members expressed through countless messages of thanks for the huge contributions they made to the successful war effort.

The sterling work of the WLA was remembered by Hampshire's National Farmers' Union members over twenty years later. When the start of the Second World War was imminent, they acknowledged that WLA members had 'proved their usefulness during the last war … paid tribute to the work women did on farms during the Great War', and asserted that 'there were few jobs on a farm that women cannot do as efficiently as men'.[4] That comment was significant as some Hampshire farmers had expressed disquiet, especially in the early First World War years, and it could be that the lesser reluctance between 1939 and 1945 was because the NFU had publicly referred to the positive contributions WLA members had made to the successful war effort.

By November 1918, over 113,000 women and girls had worked for the WLA on a full-time or a part-time basis at some point in the war years, supplemented by Italian and a smaller number of German prisoners of war, about 200 conscientious objectors and, at harvest times, schoolboys. By October 1919, though, while the need for female labour on farms was still evident, WLA membership had shrunk from a peak of 23,000 to only 8,000 when it was announced that the WLA would be demobilised on 30 November 1919. Meriel Talbot, its director since inception, wrote to members in mid-October 1919, to explain that 'now that so many men have returned from the Army it would no longer be right to spend public money on the equipping and transport of the Land Army'.[5] Each WLA member would receive a 'Certificate of Discharge on Demobilisation'.

As the last day of November approached, many closing events and church services expressed gratitude for the WLA's dedication. The largest national Farewell Rally was at Draper's Hall, London, on 27 November 1919, consisting of presentations, a supper and a concert. While its valuable work was not forgotten after its demobilisation, there were expressions of frustration and sadness at its demise. One Hampshire newspaper recorded:

how magnificently the women who enrolled in the Land Army have worked, and there will be regret throughout the county that the system is to lose its official recognition … it is certain of course that many women having a taste for the free and open life of the countryside will 'carry on' in a career which appealed to so many.[6]

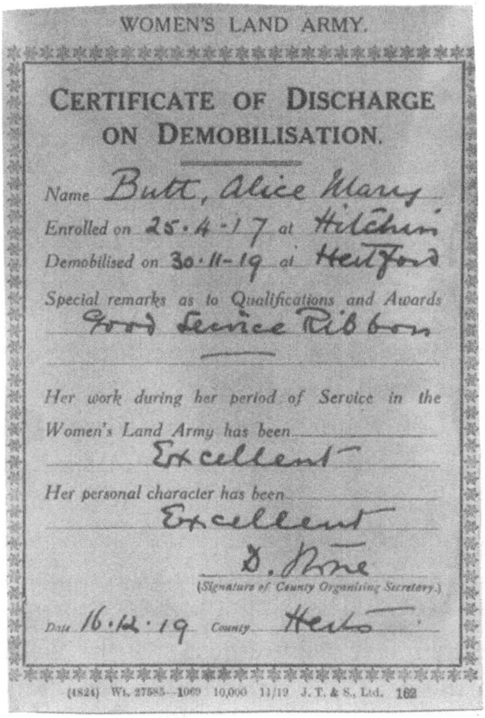
WOMEN'S LAND ARMY.

CERTIFICATE OF DISCHARGE ON DEMOBILISATION.

Name Butt, Alice Mary

Enrolled on 25.4.17 at Hitchin

Demobilised on 30.11.19 at Hertford

Special remarks as to Qualifications and Awards Good Service Ribbon

Her work during her period of Service in the Women's Land Army has been Excellent

Her personal character has been Excellent

D. [illegible]

(Signature of County Organising Secretary.)

Date 16.12.19 County Herts

(4824) Wt. 27585—1069 10,000 11/19 J. T. & S., Ltd. 162

Certificate of Discharge on Demobilisation.

Many local farewell occasions were organised, a significant number of them on the Isle of Wight. Six months after the war ended, twenty-one WLA members received the coveted 'Good Service Ribbons' from Gertrude Perrott at a ceremony at the Town Hall, Ryde.[7] Later in 1919, 150 former members met at a gathering presided over by Rev. Dr Lewen Tugwell, chairman of the island's War Sub-Committee. Tugwell was a well-known island church figure, rector of Calbourne and Rural Dean for West Wight's Church of England parishes since 1918, appointed archdeacon in 1922, and regularly involved in unveiling war memorials. When his health deteriorated, he retired to Padstow, Cornwall, where he died in October 1937.

As early as January 1916, an article in the *Hampshire Advertiser* had predicted that many women would wish to continue their wartime employment, in Britain or abroad. It said:

> a good many Englishwomen are now working in farms and gardens, to free men for their military duty, and those who find the life congenial will be specially tempted to 'trek', when peace is signed, to the great farming countries overseas.[8]

Work abroad was officially promoted to offset an agreement made in May 1919 with trade unions 'that women would not continue to work in trades after the war which prior to the war had been solely men's trades'.[9] The National Federation of Discharged Sailors and Soldiers[10] organised a march in Gosport in August 1919 with 300 unemployed ex-servicemen taking part. While the demonstration was not directed specifically at WLA members, it was hoped that 'women could now show their patriotism by giving up their war-time positions'[11] to allow those who had returned from the carnage of war to find gainful employment.

Despite the wishes of trade unions, many women who took up farming under the auspices of the WLA did decide to make it their profession when the war ended. It was noted that 'there was now more land under cultivation, and women who are really capable will be kept on. They have proved themselves especially successful as milkers and thatchers.'[12] A 1919 Hampshire report noted that, 'at least 75% of the women who were in the Land Army on demobilisation are remaining on farms,' and another stated that the same percentage would 'refuse to go back, [to previous roles] preferring the outdoor life to anything the town can offer'.[13] Warsash parish councillors were told that, 'many individual workers will continue their agricultural pursuits.'[14] A steady stream of women who had previously worked for farmers established their own smallholdings, sometimes encouraged by landowners who were prepared to rent or lease part of their farms. One Hampshire farmer was delighted that he would 'never again have a man to look after his poultry'.[15]

An extensive article in the August 1919 edition of *The Landswoman* gave information and advice to women who wished to take advantage of the assurance by the Board of Agriculture that smallholdings would be provided for those who wished to acquire one. The government's

Land Army Settlement Scheme was established to support former WLA members, an important purpose of which was to smooth the path for those with ambition to become commercial providers of food. The article drew attention, though, to difficulties in finding suitable land, building a cottage bearing in mind shortages of building materials, and delays in getting formal approval to take possession of a smallholding. Three different means for women to stay in farming were highlighted:

> (1) as a paid labourer with a cottage … for any farmer who is willing to engage her … (2) as a worker on a Profit-Sharing Farm … will earn the ordinary weekly local wage and *in addition* to their wages, at the end of the year will receive a share of the profits of the farm … (3), either as individual small holders under the County Councils or as members of one of the Board's Small Holding Co-operative Colonies.[16]

Vol. II., No. 8 AUGUST, 1919

THE LANDSWOMAN

The Journal of the Land Army and Every Country Woman

Editorial Office: Stone Field, Kidbrook Grove, Blackheath, S.E. Advertising Offices: W. H. Smith & Son, Stamford Street, S.E.1

**Land Settlement for L.A.A.S.**

LAND ARMY girls who intend to remain on the land after the demobilisation of the Land Army, and it is to be hoped there will be a great many, are no doubt beginning to think they would like to know "all about it."

Most members of the Land Army have heard by now that the Board of Agriculture has decided that the same advantages are to be given to the ex-Land Army girl as to the ex-soldier or sailor, both in the way of providing land and cottages and in making loans of capital where necessary for stocking and equipment.

The Bill at present before the House of Commons asking for these facilities has not yet been passed by Parliament and become an "Act of Parliament"—and until this has been done many of the details of the Land Settlement Scheme cannot be finally decided upon. Intending settlers should realise this and know that in a big scheme of this kind a certain

The Sower (from Millet's famous picture) [Daily News.

The future is in the hands of the woman: What will she sow?

*The Landswoman*, August 1919. The wording reads: 'The future is in the hands of the woman: What will she sow?'

The sizes of holdings were expected to be between 5 and 50 acres with a minimum capital of £150 being required for stock and equipment. In addition, prospective tenants were told of 'the necessity for having a sum of money sufficient to cover the cost of living during the first year'.[17]

Sadly, economic conditions for many sectors, including agriculture, deteriorated after the war and many smallholdings soon became unviable. With the removal of wartime price controls on basic products, prices rose by 50 per cent between April 1919 and April 1920, leading to the government imposing additional taxes in efforts to curb inflation. That, in turn, resulted in high levels of unemployment that eventually led to reduced demand and, eventually, a fall of about 25 per cent in wholesale prices between 1921 and 1929. And then through most of the 1930s there were years of recession, and social unrest in several parts of the country. All in all, the years from 1918 did not constitute an ideal period for women to be attempting to establish new, small agricultural businesses.

It is possible to make a tentative observation about the numbers of women and girls working on Hampshire farms in the years before demobilisation in November 1919. Specific figures mentioned in local newspapers were 200 in mid-1915 and 2,378 in June 1916. Using the pattern of statistics quoted for national membership in the four war years, it is conceivable that Hampshire's WLA membership may have peaked at around 3,500 in mid-1918. Assuming that figure is reasonably accurate, that would have constituted around 15 per cent of the national 23,000 figure when the war ended. If so, Hampshire could indeed have been England's largest county contributor in the recruitment and placing of women and girls.

The National Association of Landswomen had been set up after demobilisation to enrol former WLA members. It contributed to the establishment of a health insurance scheme, agitated for standardised higher wages, gave monetary support to those unable to afford agricultural and horticultural training, and provided loans for the acquisition of smallholdings. It held its first council meeting in December 1919 in the boardroom of the Agricultural Wages Board in London. There were already 6,100 members, including Mary 'Kitty' Cook, Hampshire's Organising WLA secretary, and a Mrs Dudgeon, as representatives respectively for Hampshire and the Isle of Wight. The early growth in membership quickly faded, though, and it was disbanded in 1923.

For those who did not wish, or were unable, to continue farm employment, generous assistance was stated to be available. However, the deterioration in the country's economic position during the 1920s and 1930s was not conducive to the successful finding of alternative employment. While an official claim insisted that when hostels were closed in 1919 and farm employment ceased, 'special care will be taken that no one is left stranded',[18] representations were later made arguing that payments of 15/- per week did not adequately reflect the value of WLA contributions. High and rising unemployment, among other economic problems, created severe difficulties in trying to support women to obtain civilian jobs. The reduced numbers working on farms, coupled with the compulsory conscription of more men until 1920, because of concerns about potential trouble spots in some British Empire countries and parts of mainland Europe, prompted a parliamentary motion complaining that 'having dispersed the Women's Land Army, the government propose [*sic*] still further to deplete the labour force in agriculture by a calling up of agricultural workers'.[19]

Retrospective references to the First World War appeared many years later. In February 1940, the political correspondent of the *Portsmouth Evening News* wrote in colourful language about WLA's pivotal role twenty-five years earlier:

> Every class of girl was forthcoming; the frail little typist … the lithe-limbed hockey girl straight from school … and the robust domestic … were supremely happy in the knowledge that they were 'doing their bit' for their country.[20]

'Doing their bit' involved sacrifice that was not, however, properly recognised until the twenty-first century.

# 6

# Postscript

If the women and girls who completed their service with the WLA and other wartime occupations envisaged a return to a normal life, on farms or elsewhere, many were bitterly disappointed. Married women must have been constantly worried about the whereabouts and well-being of their husbands, and such concerns were to become fully justified as ¾ million men who joined the British armed forces lost their lives in the fighting, and a similar number returned home seriously physically or mentally incapacitated. In addition to those huge numbers, the 'Spanish Flu' pandemic that reached the United Kingdom in May 1918, thought to be brought by soldiers returning home from France, resulted in the deaths of another 228,000, mainly young adults aged between 20 and 30. As for younger Hampshire girls, there was a chilling message. The senior mistress of Bournemouth High School for Girls 'stood in front of the assembled sixth form and announced to her hushed audience: only one out of ten of you can ever hope to marry. This is not a guess of mine. It is a statistical fact.'[1]

Another social consequence of the war was an almost six-fold increase in the divorce rate in England and Wales. From a relatively static annual figure of around 600 between 1900 and 1913, 3,500 divorces were granted in 1921, a number that reduced to about 2,500 each year before gradually rising again in the period leading up to the Second World War. Many possible reasons are given by historians and social scientists; the infidelity of women while their husbands were away from home, and the propensity of some men to visit brothels on mainland Europe leading to more instances of venereal diseases,[2] were two. The same pattern was apparent in other European countries and the USA.

Other causes for the increased number of divorces after 1918 were said to be tensions that arose when women no longer wished to meet the previously accepted requirements of husbands to undertake full-time home-based duties. 'While some women returned to the domestic sphere in the years following the war … an appreciable proportion of them refused to go back to full-time housekeeping and their traditional roles.'[3] Furthermore, the large rise in unemployment which, by 1921, was 12 per cent and grew throughout the 1920s, peaking at over 20 per cent in 1931 and 1932, the impact of demobilisation and the subsequent integration into civilian life of about 3.8 million men returning from war service, and housing shortages resulting in many married couples having to live in inadequate accommodation or with parents or relatives,[4] were all further factors in making the 1920s and 1930s difficult decades to find rewarding employment and social contentment.

A philosophical observation twenty years later claimed that wartime work by women led to 'the opening of the labour market and of other opportunities for which women suffragettes had long and vainly laboured'.[5] Arguably, the most important objective sought by women before the war was the achievement of greater rights, notably the ability to vote. Although women over 30 years of age who met the property qualification were entitled to participate in the December 1918 general election, it was another ten years before they gained equal voting rights with men. While it is not possible to judge the extent to which social and political progress achieved by women was helped by the valuable role they played in the war, it might well have played a significant part. The contributions that WLA members made to the substantial increase in food production cannot be over-exaggerated. They worked very long hours with little recreational time, undertook unfamiliar, often hard physical duties in strange surroundings, usually a long way from their homes in, at times, adverse weather conditions, and earned little money.

Notwithstanding Hampshire's leading role in attracting candidates to serve the WLA, and the county's farmers' eventual recognition that women were perfectly able to make vital contributions to the nation's food production, the county was far slower than others to continue that momentum. Those who might have been advocating the appointment of women to senior positions in Hampshire's public sector after the war ended needed much patience. Nancy, Viscountess Astor, had been the first woman to take a seat in parliament following her by-election victory as Conservative Member for Plymouth in November 1919, but another forty-one years elapsed before Petersfield's constituents chose a Conservative, Joan Quennell, as their MP in 1960. And forty more years passed before Sandra Gidley was elected as the Liberal Democrat member for Romsey in 2000. In local government, Hampshire residents had to wait until 1988 before a woman, Sue M. Bartlett, was elected to chair Hampshire County Council, and to 2021 before Carolyn Williamson was the first woman to be appointed its chief executive.

Finally, the end of hostilities did not, regrettably, result in long-term universal restoration of contented and ordered lives – another painful reminder that the formal cessation of war does not automatically lead to international peace, harmony and cooperation. Twenty-one years later, women and girls would, once again, be called upon to replace men on Britain's farms.

# Part 2:

# Second World War, 1939–1945

# 7

# Introduction

If the British government was slow off the mark to effectively address the consequences of the departure of men to fight in the First World War, that was not the case by the time the Second World War started in September 1939. In addition to the huge numbers of young men who joined the armed forces, others left their land-based jobs for higher wages in construction projects, building camps, aerodromes and other military establishments. An announcement inviting applications for enrolment into the re-established Women's Land Army (WLA) was issued seven months earlier in February. By early June, 8,000 expressions of interest had been received and, encouragingly, another 5,000 volunteers were going through the selection process. Even so, one branch of Hampshire's NFU complained that insufficient urgency was being shown. While acknowledging that preparations were under way, the concern was that 'the Government did not appear to train the volunteers'.[1] In February 1939, that was a correct assessment as, in a reversal of the government's decision in 1915, the initial intention was that farmers, not training institutions, would provide the essential practical instruction.

There was another problem that the government addressed much more quickly than in the First World War. Rationing then was delayed until 1918, only ten months before the war ended. In October 1939, in an attempt to significantly increase home food production, farmers were offered £2 for each acre of grassland ploughed up. However, despite the prospect of significant quantities of additional arable and horticultural land being available for cultivation, the Ministry for Food had announced in early September 1939 that rationing was likely within a few months. On 8 January 1940, with the aim of ensuring fair distribution of scarce food stocks, limits were placed on the amounts of bacon, butter and sugar that could be bought. Meat was added to the rationed food list in March, with sales of cooking fats and tea restricted in September 1940. In anticipation of the rationing, each household had to register with a named grocer in November 1939, by which time all districts were to have established Food Control Committees. To reduce the risk of profiteering, price controls were introduced. Home-grown fruit and vegetables, though, remained available without formal limitations, although in variable quantities, throughout the war years. Some controls remained in place for nine years after 1945, the United Kingdom being the last major country to completely remove rationing. Meat was the final food product to be relatively freely available in 1954, following bread in 1948, tea in 1952, and sugar and butter in 1953.[2]

The context and impact that recruits, universally known as 'land girls', had can be judged by statistics for WLA membership between 1939 and disbandment in 1950. From an initial slow uptake of recruits, 2,000 having enrolled by November 1939, greater progress was achieved in subsequent years. A total of 11,700 had joined by the end of 1940, the first full year of the war, when it was estimated that one-third of the volunteers were from London and large cities. Membership continued to increase substantially for next three years to 21,900, 53,000 and to 87,000 in 1943. Then, resulting from reduced recruitment efforts, numbers fell for the remainder of the period: 47,861 in 1944, and 43,124 in 1945. In that year, around 20 per cent of all farm work was done by prisoners of war, largely Italians but with a significant number of Germans. Governmental pressure to increase home food production continued beyond the war years, but WLA membership continued to fall steadily, to 11,210 in 1949, and 6,824 when the WLA was formally demobilised on 30 November 1950.[3]

There is evidence that Hampshire was, once again, in the forefront of the recruitment and employment of land girls. A meeting of the War Executive Committee of Hampshire's NFU in November 1939 commented on successful recruitment: 'in this respect Hampshire was the most advanced county in the whole country'.[4] Five months later it was claimed that there were 'more land girls in Hampshire than in any other county in England'.[5] Certainly, statistics issued, and statements made at intervals throughout the war, confirmed the county's substantial contribution to the overall recruitment of land girls.

# 8

# Early Women's Land Army Training at the County Farm Institute, Sparsholt

In early 1939, Hampshire County Council formed a Women's Land Army Committee with Laura Joan Chute appointed 'chairman'. She was the wife of Charles Lennard Chute, who had been a Hampshire county councillor since 1925, served as chairman of the council and the 'War Ag' committee throughout the war years. Laura Chute had held other prominent positions; she was a member of the War Pensions Committee until it was disbanded in 1922, 'chairman' of the Hampshire Nursing Association and, along with her husband, was also a member of the 'War Ag' committee. She was closely involved with the governance of what had, by 1939, become known as the Farm Institute, Sparsholt.

Laura Chute eventually passed over her WLA responsibility to Pauline Woolmer White in July 1942. Woolmer White had been a committed advocate of the WLA throughout the First World War and was also, effectively, a governor of the Farm Institute. Frequently asked to plan and support recruitment drives for WLA recruits, she organised a large one in Portsmouth in 1940, and gave much time and energy throughout the years of both wars. She died at her home at Rowland Castle in 1980, aged 88.

Every principal of English and Welsh farm training institutions had, in April 1939, received a letter from the headquarters of the County Councils Association requiring them to prepare training schemes for large numbers of land girls. The Farm Institute at Sparsholt was one of twenty-six land-based colleges in England and Wales that would be obliged, if called upon, to discontinue their normal curriculum. Major Lindsay Troup, Hampshire's Agricultural Organiser, and a past Sparsholt principal, was made aware that the government's national target for enrolment of land girls was to be at least 50,000. He had to forewarn county council members that 'the County Farm Institute could not undertake training of such women in large numbers, although it could be switched over no doubt to war requirements in case of emergency'.[1] This was an understandable reaction, as since its move from Old Basing in 1914, Sparsholt's residential accommodation could only cater for a maximum of forty students at any one time.

The government had quickly changed its mind about the arrangements for the instruction of women. In June 1939, three months before the Second World War began, the Ministry of Agriculture and Fisheries issued a directive that Sparsholt's staff were to provide '(a) training in tractor driving and (b) agricultural work'.[2] What was to be included in 'agricultural work' varied according to the season of the year. As the Farm Institute was already a long-standing land-based training facility, suitable revised arrangements could easily be made. Three one-week tractor training courses were provided, the first starting on 8 August 1939 with the other two in mid-September. In all, though, just fourteen women, two of them married, received instruction on those three courses, most of them coming from Surrey rather than Hampshire, and all paying £2 or £1/5/- for the week's tuition. Four-week general agricultural course programmes started on 11 September 1939, beginning with forty-two recruits, although a few dropped out partway through the training. New courses began each Monday and by the end of October 1939 over 100 WLA recruits had successfully completed the programmes.[3]

A 'Register' of the civilian population of England and Wales, akin to the ten-yearly population censuses but without recording places of birth, was undertaken on 29 September 1939, supervised by 65,000 enumerators. One purpose was to prepare for the issue of identity cards to adults of the two countries and, from January 1940, ration books. From the register entries, a great deal can be gleaned about the WLA recruits undertaking training and being accommodated at Sparsholt's Farm Institute. On registration day, less than a month after the Second

World War began, thirty-six trainees were resident, their ages ranging from 17 to 43. Another three students attended the course, travelling from their homes or living locally. Unlike the recruits in the First World War, who were predominantly teenagers or in their early twenties, the average age was about 25. Twenty-six of them were in their twenties, ten in their thirties, one aged 43, and just eight being younger than 20. All but four trainees were unmarried and came from a wide range of occupational backgrounds; fourteen had office-based jobs, six undertook 'unpaid domestic duties', three were 'riding school instructresses', three were parlourmaids or the equivalent, two were students, two were hairdressers, two were dressmakers, and the others were engaged in a variety of employment positions. Perceived wisdom was that few of the early women volunteering to be instructed in land-based work arrived with much knowledge of rural life or farming, an impression confirmed by knowledge of the occupations of those at Sparsholt in September 1939. Because of that, the training programmes were designed to take the lack of farm experience into account.

Without a Director of Education of the standing of David Cowan, the task of planning the curriculum fell to two very experienced men. Major Lindsay Troup had been principal at Sparsholt from 1921 to 1927 before being appointed Agricultural Adviser to Hampshire County Council, a full-time post he held until 1948. He was joined by Ronald Harris Smith, who had become the Farm Institute's principal in 1933 after the sudden departure of Troup's successor after only a short period in office. Smith had already successfully guided the Farm Institute through the intensely difficult agricultural recession and was to cope extremely well with the challenges of the six war years. Troup and Smith, aged 33 and 31 respectively when they became the Institute's principals, went on to have noteworthy careers after they left Sparsholt. Troup was later awarded an OBE for his services to local government and agricultural education, and Smith spent most of the last thirty years of his life residing on the Isle of Wight. Before his retirement at the age of 75, he held the tenancy of a large farm, served as an independent county councillor, and was closely involved with several other organisations, including the island's further education college. Smith, and his wife, Ada, had a special commitment to the Society of Friends movement, playing a pivotal role in establishing, and financially supporting, a Quaker Meeting House at Newport.[4]

Depending on the nature of the tuition given, most courses lasted four weeks, with a few of three or five weeks' duration.[5] There were, at this time, other land-based colleges in England, but three-quarters of the students coming to Sparsholt during the war came from homes outside Hampshire's county boundary.[6] The basic instruction centred around the most common jobs on farms, working with livestock, especially cows, and producing a wide range of crops, notably grain, fruit and vegetables. In 1939, milking machines were beginning to be used in greater numbers and Sparsholt's students appreciated the opportunity of learning to milk by hand and by machine.

From June 1940 until September 1944, the entire Sparsholt curriculum was devoted to training those selected to join the WLA together, from mid-1941, with a small number of boys under the age of conscription and a few men with a conscientious objection to fighting. For the Farm Institute's instruction to be fully effective, in addition to carefully worked out programmes of study and well-chosen land girl recruits, expertise and commitment of staff were essential. In that regard, Hampshire County Council's education and agriculture departments that, between them, had ultimate responsibility for the Institute's training, faced one continuous major staffing problem. Ronald Smith's leadership from the time he arrived from Derbyshire in 1933 was outstanding. He succeeded in increasing the annual student intake, notwithstanding the recession that adversely affected farming employment prospects, facilitated the elimination of financial deficits, and was later meticulous in writing letters of condolence to the families of Sparsholt students killed in the war.

Smith could not, though, control the adverse impact of high staff turnover when younger staff members were forced to resign, giving very little notice, to join the armed forces. Apart from his long-serving deputy, Captain Oswald Anderson, vice principal and warden, who returned to the Institute in 1945 following service with the RGS Territorial Army, and who stayed for another eighteen years before his retirement in 1963, almost all Sparsholt's male teaching staff had to leave for war service and did not return, resulting in training being inevitably disrupted.

Tractor Driving. (Sparsholt College Library archive)

Ploughing with horses. (Sparsholt College Library archive)

A Sparsholt bull. (Sparsholt College Library archive)

Horticultural students with the apple harvest. (Sparsholt College Library archive)

One of them, Michael Greenhill, joined the staff in September 1939 to teach, principally, tractor driving and the care of horses, but resigned in June 1942 to serve with the British army in India. Following his wartime service, Greenhill farmed in South Devon until his retirement in 1994. During his time at Sparsholt he wrote the highly respected *A Book of Farmcraft* that sold 40,000 copies. In it he noted that many WLA recruits 'had never done any work with their hands before, were completely ignorant of country ways, and needed to be given a start to their education'.[7] For inclusion in his book, Greenhill commissioned many illustrations from Evelyn Dunbar, a woman who spent much time at Sparsholt, and who became a famous wartime artist.[8]

Roger Folley came to Sparsholt from university in 1938 as the costing officer and undertook some lecturing on financial matters, but departed in August 1940 to begin training to become a flying officer. In September 1939, there were three dairying instructors teaching land girls, but the two female trainers left in 1941 to be married, and the male tutor was called up in the same year. Captain E. Jack Tredwell, the highly regarded beekeeping instructor, also had to leave to join the army but, like Anderson, resumed his appointment after the war.

The serious shortages were partially solved by appointing students to the teaching staff as soon as they completed their courses. One of them, José Loosemore, recorded that she 'had been one of the last full-time students that fateful summer of 1939, and when my training finished, I was asked to join the staff in late 1940 as an assistant dairy instructive'.[9] As a student she was 'helped to cope with being a teenager in an adult world'[10] and recalled that most WLA volunteers were 'town girls, never having seen milk other than in bottles on door-steps … quickly learnt how to scrub milk buckets and churns'.[11] Other assistance was provided by retired staff who returned to replace colleagues who were called up. One of them, Harold Young, first appointed to Sparsholt in 1920, quickly gained an enviable reputation in apiary circles in Hampshire and further afield, and came to the Institute's aid again by resuming beekeeping tuition until Tredwell returned.

Despite a smaller pool of experienced instructors, for several years an increasing number of WLA recruits passed through Sparsholt. The *Student Register* showed 143 women and girls completing courses in 1940, 184 in 1941, 172 in 1942, and 208 in 1943. In addition to their teaching commitments, Sparsholt staff supported national efforts to address food shortages caused by the impact of rationing of most products. Many met regularly with Hampshire's gardening and allotment societies to give lectures and talks focusing on ways of growing more food items. One of them, Miss Britles, regularly gave demonstrations from 1940 onwards to groups of women on the subject of 'substitutes for rationed food'.[12] The Upham branch of the Women's Institute met with her in April that year, and many other groups received visits. Institute staff used their links with local groups to emphasise and reinforce the government's 'Dig for Victory' campaign to encourage the expansion of allotments and public spaces to support the aim of producing more home-grown food.

The efforts made by Sparsholt's WLA recruits were greatly appreciated by the instructors. One senior staff member, E.J. Bullock, superintendent in charge of all the work undertaken by trainees, said that 'they do all the average heavy work of a farm within reason and can stay the time as well as any farm labourer'.[13] A wide variety of specialist opportunities were offered to those on the four-week courses, including thatching, hedging and, when poor weather intervened, repairing equipment.[14]

# 9

# Women's Land Army Members' Experience in Hampshire, 1939–1942

By the end of November 1939, 207 women and girls had already been placed on Hampshire's farms, although Sparsholt had instructed fewer than half that number. The county's WLA committee updated the position in January 1940 when there were '609 active members on the register; 42 volunteers had received college training and 137 had received training on an approved farm … The remaining volunteers will be called up when they are needed.'[1]

Some land girls who worked in Hampshire came great distances. One such was Isabella Waddell, who left her parents' farm at Dunfermline, Fife, and settled near Stockbridge with her brother who was waiting to be sent abroad with the armed forces. When he was given his posting date, he encouraged his sister to find a job helping the war effort and accompanied Isabella to the WLA recruiting office in Stockbridge town centre. Her application was successful, and her membership card gives the joining date as 25 July 1940. Isabella's entry in *World War II Women's Land Army Index Cards 1939–1948* shows that she began employment on 7 July 1941 and left on 'Medical Grounds' on 13 January 1944. On 28 July 1941, Isabella began a five-week course, costing £6/5/-, at Sparsholt's Farm Institute. She kept a notebook that described some of the things she was taught which showed the diligence with which she undertook her studies. One entry reads, 'a two furrow tractor plough should do ½ acre an hour', on another page there are drawings made after a 'lecture on Internal Combustion Engine', and she records the award to her of the 'National Diploma Agric.

BSc (AGRI)'. Isabella married John Parrington in November 1942 and after leaving the WLA in January 1944, she became, as many land girls did, a farmer's wife, at Woodcote Farm, Upham.[2]

Hampshire's position as a front runner in the recruitment of land girls was evident in employment statistics for numbers working on farms in English counties in April 1940. There were already 307 land girls working in Hampshire, more than the combined figures for West and East Sussex, and 25 per cent more than in Kent, the next highest county.[3] By the end of that year, only Yorkshire, a much larger county, had more than the 421 working in Hampshire, including the Isle of Wight, a number that had increased to 600 by mid-1941. In August that year, Lady Denman, Honorary Director of the WLA, in a speech at The Vyne, Basingstoke, the home of Charles and Laura Chute, 'congratulated Hampshire on being the second most successful county in England'.[4]

In addition to its vital training responsibilities, Sparsholt's Farm Institute was a working farm. Anne Hall, taken on as a temporary employee in October 1940, was appointed to the permanent staff a year later, being paid £1/15/- per week. She described her experience as a land girl in detail: to be ready to start work at 7 a.m., she was normally out of bed at 6 a.m., except when morning milking was part of her duties when the alarm was sounded at 4.30 a.m. There was three-quarters of an hour allocated for breakfast, one-hour breaks for lunch and tea in late afternoon, then the evening milking commitment, before land girls were allowed to leave the farm on the strict condition that they returned by 10 p.m. Hall had a wide variety of jobs to undertake, depending on the season. Potato picking, raking up couch grass, renewing pig fencing, milking, harvesting sugar beet, working with pigs, horses, and the relatively new threshing machines, were examples of her duties.[5] She worked at the institute until July 1942 before moving to Clanville Lodge, a farm near Andover.

More farmers were required to come forward to give instruction as the Farm Institute could not meet the increasing demand for labour. As well as capacity issues at Sparsholt, there were other reasons for training being delivered on farms and not in college settings. The cost of providing tuition was one factor. Sir Reginal Dorman-Smith, MP for Petersfield since 1935, and president of both the NFU and the Ministry of Agriculture, was a man whose views were widely respected. He knew Sparsholt's Farm Institute well and appreciated its training capability, but claimed in the House of Commons that a recruit trained on a farm would cost £5 for four weeks, only half the cost of a training institution.[6] Another advocate of giving instruction to recruits on farms rather than in colleges was the chairman of the NFU's Alton branch, who commented that it was 'better if farmers trained the land girls on their own farms as the commercial side of farming was not much considered in the colleges'.[7]

A second inhibiting factor was that Sparsholt staff were not able to meet all Hampshire's needs. It could not satisfy the demand for women and girls to undertake tree-felling work in the New Forest so that the timber could be used for 'pit props and helping in the charcoal industry'.[8] The charcoal obtained when wood was burnt was used in the manufacture of ammunition. A separate forestry section was formed in 1942, the members being known as 'lumber Jills', with training provided by specialist staff. On the other hand, one important specialist subject that was taught at Sparsholt was the 'hitherto jealously-guarded secret of thatching',[9] a skill required to meet a large number of tasks.

'Members of the Women's Land Army being instructed in the art of thatching.' (Getty Images, serial no.1297440939; photo by Reg Speller)

Demand for volunteers to come forward to work on Hampshire's farms after most male workers had left to join the armed forces normally continued to outstrip supply. Under headings such as 'More Vacancies than Volunteers', local newspapers reported in April 1940 that Hampshire needed 350 more full-time workers and, for the first time, people were sought who could only 'spare a month or so'.[10] A few weeks later, the vacancy number had risen to 400. Perhaps anticipating problems in satisfying forthcoming labour shortages, Lindsay Troup, Hampshire's Agricultural Organiser, had urged farmers several months earlier to plan for the future grain harvest, and to advise the 'War Ag' committee of their expected requirements, telling them that workers for dairying and horticultural activities were in particularly short supply. Some papers quoted a comment from a Ministry of Agriculture leaflet published in October 1940: 'Without the food you help to provide, the bravery of the fighting services would be of no avail and the machinery in our munition factories would be silent and still.'[11]

By early 1941, it was evident that additional resource would be needed at harvest times. Supplementing WLA work, residential Volunteer Agricultural Camps for schoolboys between the ages of 14½ and 18 were designed to help farmers pick strawberries, raspberries and other important Hampshire crops during their summer holiday. In 1940, Canon Spencer Leeson, headmaster of Winchester College and chairman of the Headmasters' Conference, decided that some senior college students would undertake summer labouring work, a role quite unfamiliar to the majority of them. In the same year, boys from Regents Park School, Southampton, attended a local harvest camp working for thirty hours a week, and in 1941 students from Dulwich College, London, camped and worked on farms around Stockbridge.

While the subsequent career progressions of most WLA members were not publicly recorded, one land girl did become a notable figure in Hampshire farming circles. Maureen De Rougemont, born to a French mother and Swiss father in January 1923, was educated in England and at the onset of the war joined the WLA in Dorset. She soon moved to Hampshire, where she worked on three farms, subsequently, on her departure from the WLA in 1945, buying Bigpath Farm, Upham, at that time comprising 88 acres and two cottages. After her marriage to Thomas Barr, a Scottish-born vet, and in addition to running her farm, she became involved in several agricultural-based organisations, including as an advisory member of Winchester's Young Farmers' Club, a member of Southampton June Dairy Festival, and the south-east Hampshire Smallholdings Committees. Maureen Barr became a prominent figure in the NFU, serving as vice 'chairman' of the Winchester branch before being appointed the first woman 'chairman' of the Hampshire County NFU Executive in 1961.

Although the need for ever more land girls was evident, the selection process was extremely thorough, and there was no disguising the expectations required of WLA members. Both sides of the membership card spelt out what the land girls were agreeing to provide. 'You have made the home fields your battlefield. Your country relies on your loyalty and welcomes your help' was the third commitment made on the face of the card, and the reverse included an agreement that land girls must seek 'permission to resign if circumstances arise which make it difficult to keep her promise of service' and 'must not resign until this permission is received'. If and when a land girl was allowed to leave, 'she must return her uniform and badge to the county Land Army office'.[12]

The particular features of the soil and climate in south-east Hampshire were favourable for the growing of strawberries. A large number of seasonal employees were required to pick the crops over a short season, and E.M. Biggs, manager of Solent Court Farm, a Warsash strawberry grower, expressed his appreciation in 1940 that land girls working on his farm had come from all over the country. Many came from London with no previous experience of farm work, with others arriving from Devon to pick for a few weeks before that county's crop was ready for harvesting. Biggs was grateful that 'they sleep under canvas in a large field and work nine or ten hours daily'[13] without making any fuss. There were, though, jobs that land girls did regard as unpleasant. Working in sugar beet fields and with threshing machines were often most disliked; one was back-breaking, and the other caused a huge amount of dust that was distinctly uncomfortable to endure.

At the start of 1941, Laura Chute, 'chairman' of Hampshire's WLA committee, in an open letter, urged 'any women between the ages of 18 and 40 who is physically fit, prepared to adapt herself to country life … should seriously consider whether enrolment in the Women's Land Army is not the best contribution she can make to the war effort'.[14]

In a follow-up appeal, she stressed that the training available was free and, furthermore, 10/- per week would be paid as pocket money.

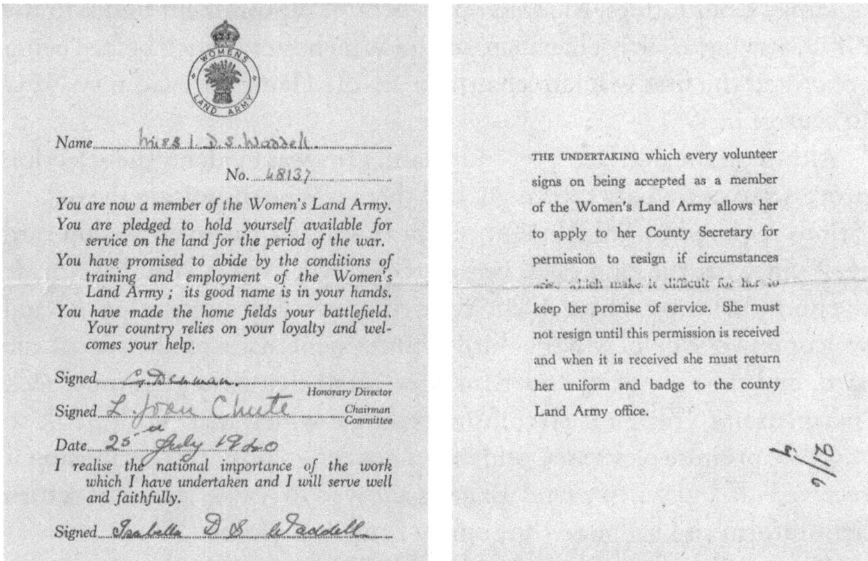

WOMEN'S LAND ARMY

Name Miss I. D. S. Waddell

No. 48137

*You are now a member of the Women's Land Army.*
*You are pledged to hold yourself available for service on the land for the period of the war.*
*You have promised to abide by the conditions of training and employment of the Women's Land Army; its good name is in your hands.*
*You have made the home fields your battlefield. Your country relies on your loyalty and welcomes your help.*

Signed C. Denman — Honorary Director

Signed L. Joan Chute — Chairman Committee

Date 25th July 1940

*I realise the national importance of the work which I have undertaken and I will serve well and faithfully.*

Signed Isabella D S Waddell

THE UNDERTAKING which every volunteer signs on being accepted as a member of the Women's Land Army allows her to apply to her County Secretary for permission to resign if circumstances arise which make it difficult for her to keep her promise of service. She must not resign until this permission is received and when it is received she must return her uniform and badge to the county Land Army office.

6/10

Women's Land Army membership card issued to Isabella D.S. Waddell, 25 July 1940 (Left: front, Right: reverse) (Reproduced with thanks to Isabella's son, John Parrington; copy provided by John Parrington)

A sign that the shortage of land girls was becoming critical was evident when a few recruits in the war's early stages were permitted to have other jobs. One such was Kathleen Horniblow, born in 1918, always known as 'Bunty', who was recorded as 'Assistant Kindergarten Mistress' in the September 1939 registration. Bunty joined the WLA soon after the war began, working in the afternoons for William H. Wroth of Horsebridge Farm, Horsebridge, situated between Stockbridge and King's Somborne, and teaching at a King's Somborne kindergarten in the mornings. She resigned from the WLA in January 1943 to continue her teaching career at St Swithuns School, Winchester, and later at Durston independent school in London.[15] In September 1941, she witnessed the demonstration of an 'Australian Sunshine stripper harvester', designed by an 18-year-old boy, Hugh McKay from Victoria, Australia. It was to cut the heads from grain

An 'Australian Sunshine Stripper harvester' being demonstrated at Mr W.H. Wroth's farm. Bunty Horniblow is the person standing on the machine. (Reproduced with thanks to Bruce and Gill Horn)

crops, and subsequent improvements led to it being successfully exported to the United Kingdom from the early 1940s.

While the main operational matter to be solved was the constant shortage of trained land girls to fill vacancies, one organisational and structural issue emerged that gave a clear indication that tensions existed among Hampshire's leadership functions. Laura Chute was at the centre of the perceived need to clarify the different roles of various officials. A letter to her from Lady Gertrude Denman's WLA headquarters at Balcombe Place, Haywards Heath, Sussex, expressed concerned about a blurring of responsibilities. Lady Denman felt it necessary to explain that the WLA was not a voluntary organisation but a 'section of a Government Department', 'salaried County Secretaries are government officials', and that Hampshire's WLA 'Committee's function is an advisory one'. The letter closed with the statement that the system is 'operating most smoothly in the very large majority of counties where the Chairman and Secretary work together as colleagues, keeping in close touch over day to day developments. I hope the same smooth working will obtain in Hampshire.'[16] It may have been no coincidence that Mrs Chute passed her chairing responsibility to Pauline Woolmer White in July 1942, less than a year later. Significantly, the letter confirming Woolmer White's appointment told her that 'the office of Women's Land Army County Chairman is by no means a sinecure'.[17]

There were two contributory reasons for the constant exhortations for more recruits from early 1942. One was that after the Pearl Harbor attack in December 1941, another 100,000 men were called up, and the other was the government's requirement that an extra 2 million acres of land should be ploughed to produce greater quantities of wheat, sugar beet and potatoes. To help achieve that objective, 3,000 Italian prisoners of war were to be available to farmers from the second half of the year. Further assistance was expected from large numbers of schoolboys and university students who would help with harvests during their summer holiday.[18] The government's pleas were remarkably successful; there were 128,000 more acres cultivated with potatoes in 1941, the crop being 92 per cent higher than in 1938. However, despite acreage under permanent grass falling by 34 per cent between 1939 and 1943, the number of WLA members who were 'milkers' had risen in 1943 to 20,159, over 25 per cent of the total membership.

While the government's target was a logical response to the urgent need for more cultivated land, some Hampshire farmers felt disadvantaged when they adhered to the imposition. There was anecdotal evidence that sheep-farming land in the west of Hampshire was found to be quite unsuitable for other uses, and farmers suffered financial losses when disappointing yields resulted from the cultivation of former pasture land for cereal crops.[19] Another example came from the Horn family farm, Hipley Farm, Hambledon, in the east of the county, where 17 acres of an 80-acre dairy farm was given over to growing wheat and oats in two successive years. 'The land was required to be ploughed up by a government initiative to help increase food production,' but part of it could get excessively wet in the winter months and excessively dry in the summer. The clay soil was so unsuitable for growing grain that in one year Sydney Horn, the farm's owner, resorted to sowing wheat seed by hand as any wheeled vehicle could well have become stuck in mud.[20]

Recruitment poster, 1941.

The demanding nature of Hampshire's selection process included the completion of five forms, one stressing that 'girls should be strong, able to undertake strenuous work, heavy lifting, and cope with an outdoor life in all weathers'. Even height was to be considered: 'short stature is a definite disadvantage and needs to be compensated by sturdiness'.[21] A handwritten note of guidance for interviewers was produced by Woolmer White. In addition to being prepared to work anywhere in the country, potential recruits had to confirm that their availability would be on a full-time basis. They were told what hours of work would be expected, what 'time-off' they would be entitled to, what their billeting arrangements would be, the content of their training, what extra clothing would be required, and warned that 'winter could at times be lonely'. Candidates were asked whether they were 'married or going to be?' The normal age of entry was 17, and if candidates were 16 years of age, confirmation of parental consent and receipt of a character reference would be necessary. Working conditions were spelt out: 'all the hardships and difficulties of country life should be explained to the volunteer: loneliness, lack of time off, primitive sanitation etc.'[22] Holiday entitlement in 1941 was extremely modest, land girls being entitled to just one day off every four months unless farmers were prepared to be more generous. Normal weekly working hours were forty-eight in the winter and fifty in summer months.

Most recruits did not work on a single farm but were placed in groups, known as 'gangs', based in a local area, usually living together in hostel accommodation. Groups sometimes contained as many as twenty-six land girls and would be part of a strict hierarchical structure. There were 'gang leaders' who reported to a 'Forewoman' who, in turn, reported to a 'Supervisor' who was accountable to a WLA committee member. Gangs were divided into smaller numbers and moved around different farms to undertake similar tasks. Examples were hoeing, harvesting and riddling of potatoes, and similar processes with flax and turnips.[23] There were also vital but less obvious tasks. Maximising yields was important, and with rats and rabbits causing damage to crops by reducing yields, some land girls were employed to try and catch and destroy them, a job they were reluctant to volunteer for. Not all produce was destined for the home market. In south Hampshire, with Southampton and Portsmouth naval ports close by, some seasonal vegetable produce was exported to feed armed forces in France.

'The Land Army Growing Vegetables for the Navy', showing a gang of land girls harvesting and packaging cabbages into wooden crates with the Isle of Wight in the background. (Picture by Archibald Standish Hartrick, courtesy of the Garden Museum)

Hampshire was divided into five regions, with a WLA committee member providing oversight for each. The 'south west' section covered the New Forest which, together with the other groups based around the 'central south', 'central east', 'central', and 'north east', formed the county's groupings. Representatives were charged with a number of tasks. They were to meet with supervisors, visit new recruits within a few days of their arrival, arrange for them to be registered with a local doctor, speak with 'gangs' once a month, provide details of libraries, canteens, and 'investigate farms and billets'.[24] Once a quarter, representatives were to submit written reports for consideration at each committee meeting. Among other things, information was to be provided about land girls who had significant illness, changed their address, left, and those who were planning to be married.

As was the case during the Great War of 1914–1918, the identification of sufficient accommodation for WLA workers created challenges.

Throughout the country, following a national drive begun in 1941 to increase the number, 696 hostels were eventually acquired to house 22,000 women and girls. Acquisitions included hotels and church rectories, and in Hampshire, to complement the use of existing large houses, new hostel buildings were to be erected to a standard design to accommodate between thirty and fifty land girls. Buildings would comprise three blocks: 'dormitories' with ten girls in each, 'ablution' areas comprising baths, washbasins, toilets, washing and drying facilities for clothes, and 'welfare' facilities with dining and recreation space.[25] Hostels, however, could not provide more than about a third of the residential accommodation needed, and incentives were offered to householders to offer a variety of billets to those land girls who were not living in hostels or the homes of their employers.

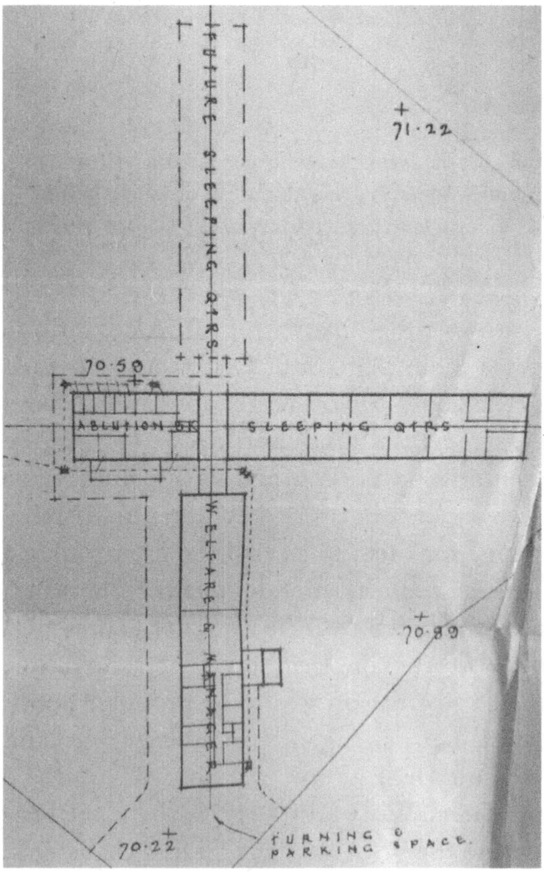


Plan for 'Agricultural Workers' Hostel' at Colden Common, Brambridge, submitted to Winchester Rural District Council, 1 August 1941, approved 28 August 1941.

Dining room at a Women's Land Army Hostel. (Painting by Evelyn Dunbar, 1943)

By 1943 there were at least seventeen hostels in Hampshire. In 1941, one was opened at Brambridge, Colden Common, capable of housing fifty land girls, after plans submitted to Winchester Rural District Council were very promptly approved on 28 August that year. Owned by the Ministry of Agriculture, it was a single-storey 'Maycrete Precast Living Hut'. The accommodation comprised space for fifty bunk beds, a 'Recreational and Dining Room', a kitchen, two bathrooms, six WC cubicles, two showers, a cycle rack, and sleeping and common room facilities for staff at one end of the building. It was situated on a private road close to Bugle Farm House and Brambridge Cottage.[26]

A similarly sized hostel at Kingsclere served farms around Basingstoke, one in Winchester Road, Bishop's Waltham, still had twenty-five residents when it was closed in 1951, and another was Brook House, Brook Lane, Botley, a Grade 2 property built in the late eighteenth century and now a Masonic Centre. At Hook, in the north-east corner of the county, a hostel was opened in September 1942 'with a full complement of 40 Hampshire girls'.[27] Standen House, Chute Standen, was a hostel close to the Hampshire/Wiltshire border, and others in the south of the county were located at Lee on Solent, Burbush House, Burley, Dock House, Beaulieu, Beech House, Holmsley, and at Curdbridge. Elsewhere, hostels were to be established at Houghton and Longstock, both near Stockbridge, closer to the centre of the county.

Much is known about one large hostel, Redenham House, Weyhill, near Andover, a substantial 'Stone-built Georgian Mansion' built in 1784. In addition to newspaper reports, surviving memoirs left by two WLA members, and a conversation with a man who has worked on the Redenham estate for nearly fifty years, have enabled a full picture to emerge. It was requisitioned for use as a hostel in late 1942 to accommodate, when fully occupied, up to 100 land girls. A brochure produced in preparation for sale of the whole estate by auction in September 1948 recorded that 'The Mansion and about 1½ acres are under requisition to the Ministry of Works at a rental of £432 p.a., and are at present used as a hostel for the Women's Land Army.'[28] The ground floor included four large 'reception' rooms; a 'Spacious Dining Room', a 'Drawing Room', a 'Boudoir or Study', and a 'Library'. Elsewhere on the ground floor were extensive facilities, collectively referred to as 'Domestic Offices'. The first floor contained eight bedrooms, many with fireplaces, four bathrooms, plus two more bedrooms, a bathroom and other rooms to accommodate 'maids'. The largest bedrooms were arranged to accommodate ten or twelve land girls in bunk beds. On a second floor, another nine smaller bedrooms and one bathroom were also used by WLA members. In addition, there was 'a large range of cellars' with rooms, store cupboards, and several boilers for central heating and 'domestic hot water'.[29]

On a Saturday afternoon in September 1946, a serious fire started in a laundry room on the top floor of the house also containing living accommodation for some of the land girls. Caused, reputably, when an iron was left on and overheated, the local fire service was alerted at 2 p.m. Fire engines were despatched from many Hampshire towns, including nearby Andover and Ludgershall, and Alresford, Basingstoke, Winchester, Southampton and Stockbridge, and as far away as Newbury and Amesbury. Water was pumped from a reservoir a mile away and in all 50,000 gallons were needed to extinguish the blaze. Two-thirds of the roof was destroyed, extensive damage was done to the top of the building, and debris and water badly affected the floors below.[30] By the autumn of 1946, the number of land girls living at Redenham House, and other hostels, had reduced and many residents were away for the weekend. On their return, they were relocated to nearby Chute House, Chute Standen, for at least a year until Redenham House had been repaired.

One of the land girls, Gwendoline (Gwen) Place found Redenham House a congenial place to live. Born in 1926, Gwen joined the WLA in 1943 at the age of 17 and arrived as one of the first ten girls from Southampton, Portsmouth and Bournemouth to take up residence at the house. She quickly made many friends and grew to have a very high regard for the strict, but fair, matron, Mrs Moyra Drake-Brockman, always simply known as 'DB'. In addition to her wide range of duties such as thatching, picking Brussels sprouts, 'cleaning out hen and chicken huts', and collecting potatoes 'thrown up by a tractor', she learned to drive a 3-tonne lorry that took land girls to and from their allocated farms, sometimes as far away as Southampton. Gwen recalled her 'gratitude that she was able to be of service to the country in such a way that she was distanced from much of the danger of war … but mostly she is grateful for the friendships she developed'. As with daughters in many other families, Gwen's parents did not wish her to join any of the fighting forces.

Gwen left the WLA in November 1949, four months after she had married Maurice Raggett. Thirty-four years later, she returned to Redenham House for a reunion of thirty-eight former land girls who had lived there for some or all the time between its opening and its closure at the end of 1948. In memory of the WLA residents, and with the full agreement of the estate's owners, Sir John and Lady Olivia Clark, Gwen and her husband went again in March 1990 to plant a tree in the grounds to the south of the house. After arranging for a memorial brass plaque mounted on a piece of Purbeck stone to be produced, she

Redenham House, Weyhill, Hampshire, circa 1945. (Lent by Redenham House staff)

Memorial tree in Redenham House grounds, planted by Gwen and Maurice Raggett.

Memorial plaque provided by Gwen Raggett in 1990, at the base of the tree.

returned to place it at the base of the tree. John Marshall, a long-serving member of Redenham's staff, made an attractive brick plinth to which the plaque was later fixed. After her WLA service, Gwen became a volunteer with the Women's Royal Voluntary Service (WRVS), and other organisations, and was awarded an MBE in 2005 for her extensive, long-term commitment to voluntary bodies.[31]

Another land girl, Betty Dannatt (née Wellings), joined the WLA in September 1943, by which time Redenham House was fully occupied. She was one of five girls who travelled to Hampshire from Walsall, Staffordshire, and recorded that:

> Redenham House was large with a long drive up to its very impressive front doors. I believe there were between 80 and 90 of us who were soon allocated our place in various bedrooms. Our room held 6 bunks, bedside cabinets and wardrobes with plenty of space between. Our bathroom was next door. There was a main Warden and two helpers, plus kitchen staff, who made us very welcome and told us what was expected of us to make sure life was well ordered, such as mealtimes and bedtimes including two late passes each week, otherwise ten o'clock meant front door closed. Breakfast was served around 7.30, we also made our own lunch packs.[32]

Not all the accommodation provided for land girls resulted from decisions made by the WLA leadership. In the grounds of Hale Nursery, near Fordingbridge in west Hampshire, a hostel was provided by the proprietor, Captain Guy Dodgson, who ran a major horticulture business, growing large quantities of lettuce, onions, tomatoes and flowers. By the start of the Second World War, over 100 staff were employed there, including, later on, at least fifteen land girls, two of whom were to marry local men. Dodgson was the son of the founder, and for several years was chairman of Hampshire's Horticultural Section of the NFU. When the war ended some land girls stayed on for a while, but the business closed in 1985, with the site later developed for housing.[33]

Hostel built for the land girls at Hale Nursery, near Fordingbridge.

Land girls in their familiar uniform at Hale Nursery, circa 1945.

Strict rules were imposed on residents of Hampshire's hostels run under the auspices of the WLA. The need for punctuality was stressed, 'intoxicating drinks may not be brought into the hostel' and those who use 'cocoa mugs at night must wash them up and return them to the kitchen'. Smoking was not allowed in dormitories, nor were candles. 'Lights out' time was 11 p.m., and residents had to return by 10.30 p.m. except on two nights, normally Saturday or Sunday and one weekday evening, when an 11 p.m. return time was permitted. Each hostel was to have a formal house committee comprising five volunteers who would meet weekly, with one person standing down every six months. Residents 'are asked to remember that a Land Army hostel arouses interest in the neighbourhood and that noisy behaviour, lingering round the entrance and acts of thoughtlessness cause general condemnation'.[34] All WLA committee members, in their capacity as hostel representatives, were responsible for those in their areas, and were to be visited weekly. They answered queries, dealt with replacement of uniforms, enquired of wardens about behaviour, took an interest in food menus, and advised land girls of any forthcoming major developments. Representatives were also specifically required to 'support WLA Rulings and Decisions about girls and staff'.[35] While restrictive conditions were imposed in hostels, they were often regarded as preferable to private billets. One land girl, Nancy Cooper, found accommodation in Hampshire farmhouses so unsuitable that she moved three times in the same area in just six months.[36]

While, in Hampshire and nationally, the supply of recruits frequently failed to match demand for women's labour, there were occasional examples of girls who had been trained at land-based institutions but could not immediately find farmers to employ them. In those circumstances, if WLA recruits had given up jobs to attend courses, they were not entitled to unemployment pay.[37] By August 1940, 8,000 WLA members were working on farms in England, and although that number had increased to 14,600 a year later, double that figure was said to be required when the call-up age for younger males was reduced. By the spring of 1940, 350 women and girls were fully employed on Hampshire farms, and as 'applications are pouring in', 'we are totally unable to cope with the demand'.[38] A further recruitment incentive to attract women up to the age of 30 came in December 1941 when a firmer policy was introduced with the passing of the National Service Act (No.2). That Act instructed women to select a national service to join, of which the WLA was one. Initially, the requirement applied to childless widows or women between the ages of 20 and 30, but the pool of workers was later greatly expanded when the age range was widened to cover those between 19 and 43.

To overcome the shortage of volunteers, various suggestions were made to expand the workforce beyond members of the WLA. One early possibility to cope with the demand for additional labour was encapsulated in a resolution passed by the Hampshire executive of the NFU in January 1940. It proposed that 'all farm workers should be exempt from military service from 18 upwards. Coal miners were exempt, so why not farmers?'[39] That proposal was not accepted by decisionmakers, and farms and Sparsholt's Farm Institute continued to lose staff to meet war service requirements. A partial solution became evident when people from urban and residential areas of the country were found to be equally capable of performing effectively in land-based jobs. An Isle of Wight farmer was moved to comment that 'city girls who have scarcely seen a farm before have, during the months they have been on the island, blossomed into a real asset in their new work'.[40] Other appreciative letters appeared in local newspapers.

To supplement the work of land girls, the Ministry of Agriculture formed the Emergency Land Corps that was to 'enrol volunteer women workers who can spare half a day a week or a weekend or a few hours now and then for such work as potato planting, hoeing roots, fruit picking, pea picking, haymaking and harvesting'.[41] The much wider acceptable age range of between 14 and 70 indicated the seriousness of the situation, and was designed to 'provide a safeguard against wastage of any food crops through lack of labour'.[42]

Doubts about the ability of land girls to adequately replace male labour had surfaced in the early war years. In January 1940, the *Daily Mail*, agitating in favour of a Youth Land Army, questioned the government's reluctance to accept the proposal. 'Is it because their Women's Land Army has been such a dismal failure?'[43] One farmer insisted to a questioner 'that the day he had a land girl on his farm would be the day he died – "bloody women"!'[44] While these were isolated adverse comments, some farmers wished to limit and restrict the number of labourers being called up to join the armed forces by expressing the view that 'the Women's Land Army did good work but there were limitations'.[45] Those 'limitations' were articulated later in 1940: 'many women cannot undertake hard and very laborious work' but 'there are a dozen jobs that girls can do on the farm',[46] and training should be concentrated on those activities. From a subjective perspective, William (Bill) Holmes, general secretary of the National Union of Agricultural Workers, said that 'it was obvious that women … could not do heavy work on the farms, such as ploughing and tractor driving'.[47] The evidence was very different.

One rarely heard reservation came from a report that employing female labour was not 'more welcome to farmers' wives, but they must make the best of the situation, which is nationally very serious, and be prepared even for further sacrifices of old prejudices'.[48] The grumbles were sufficiently frequent, wide-ranging and serious for Robert Hudson, Minister of Agriculture: 'speaking at a meeting of farmers, [he] took the opportunity to vociferously state how he deplored the present state of criticism. It was the height of folly and short-sightedness.'[49] The opposition and prejudices exhibited by farmers lessened from mid-1941 onwards.

Yet another deterrent to recruiting enough women employees on farms was the pay they received in the early war years. While rates were later increased substantially, the initial minimum wage for WLA members was £1/17/6d for a fifty-hour week, adjusted in December 1941 for those over 18 to £1/19/- with the length of the working week reduced a little to forty-eight hours. Younger workers were still paid £1/12/6d per week, with 14/- deducted if boarding accommodation and meals were provided. Even though holiday entitlement was modest in the extreme, free travel vouchers over the 1942 Christmas period were not allocated to those who wished to go home between 24 and 28 December.

Another cause for dissatisfaction was the clothing issued to land girls. Uniforms were said to be too bulky to wear in summer and insufficiently waterproof for winter weather. Another complaint was that a lack of headwear protection from summer sun brought on serious migraine attacks. On the other hand, girls working near Portsmouth were grateful that they were 'supplied with tin hats … since shrapnel sometimes fell plentifully'.[50] One land girl who served on farms around Southampton from 1942 to 1950 described her experience:

> Clothing was more difficult as although we were provided with a uniform, the breeches were not practical for dairy work and too hot too [*sic*] wear in the summer so we kept them for going out or cut them down to make shorts … The Women's Land Army were [*sic*] not forthcoming about replacing these so if we did not have enough clothing coupons to buy boots we just had wet feet. There were no waterproof jackets and the overcoats were too bulky to work in so we were wet a good deal of the time in winter.[51]

It was unlikely that the understandable reservations in the minds of potential land girls would be eased if they saw the monthly comments in *The Farmer's Calendar of Work* for 1941 or 1942. It ended with an overriding summary:

> It is hoped, however, that the new recruit who joins the Women's Land Army may, on reading this, find some solace (if she joins up at the season of hedging and ditching – or worse still, hoeing and singling) in the fact that the whole of her service in the Women's Land Army will not be spent with blistered hands pulling docks. Each month brings its own problems and its own interests.[52]

Not remarks likely to endear farm work to potential WLA land girls.

# 10

# Expansion of Women's Land Army in Hampshire, 1943–1945

At the very end of December 1942, a speech by Robert Hudson, Minister of Agriculture, contained announcements that underlined the seriousness of the potential shortfall in food production. Output, he said, would need to increase by 15 per cent in 1943, adding that there was no prospect of men in the armed forces being released from their fighting roles. That meant, he went on, that the membership of the WLA would need to be doubled to 100,000. In part, the increase followed success in ploughing another 700,000 acres for cultivation.

Despite the challenges of recruiting, training and placing adequate numbers of land girls to Hampshire's farms, regular drives to encourage additional candidates to come forward did bear fruit. Sparsholt's Farm Institute was able to train 15 per cent more students in 1943 compared with the previous year, itself the highest number achieved until then. For the start of the 1944 academic year in September, boys and girls resumed instruction on the same courses, but specific WLA training continued. Proficiency tests in the effective use of machine milking and in other farming activities were imposed before farmers had confidence that land girls were properly qualified. In April 1943, oral and practical examinations were held at Sparsholt, supervised by a member of the family that farmed Westley Farm before it was acquired by Hampshire County Council in 1912. Four candidates received honours awards and another seven gained passes.[1]

The imbalance between demand and supply for farm workers was frequently evident, but national recruitment for the WLA was controversially suspended in 1943 because shortages were particularly acute in aircraft and munition factories. That decision was not welcomed in Hampshire. The Swanwick and District Fruit Growers Association Ltd, founded in 1905, and the Wickham and District Horticultural branch of the NFU, were among bodies to protest about the inability to obtain enough labour to harvest horticultural produce. While advertisements for land girls to work on farms ceased, they continued for assistant wardens, cooks and domestic staff for Hampshire's hostels, as recruiting difficulties were frequently apparent.

By early 1943, though, the national target for WLA membership had been reached, assisted by the employment of some 20,000 prisoners of war. A considerable number were assigned to Hampshire farms, being brought from one of the county's seventeen prisoner-of-war camps. Several reports commented on the hard physical effort put in by German prisoners of war, but with the observation that they worked at the other ends of fields to land girls, and were not expected to turn out if the weather was too cold – unlike land girls, for whom there was no such respite.[2] A considerable number of former prisoners were to remain in this country after the war ended, and still more kept in contact with the farmers who provided them with work. Three such German prisoners were Walter Zimmerman, Josef Leisch and Hermann Meyer. Leisch and Meyer lived in a bungalow on Pondside Farm, Meonstoke, east Hampshire, sharing meals with Horn family members, while working six days a week. 'They benefitted from the perks of eating fresh produce Bob was growing on the farm, without the strict rationing they had experienced in the POW camp in which they had been interred.'[3]

Included in the national total of farm workers were a small number of conscientious objectors, often known as 'conchies'. Sparsholt, together with other land-based institutions, provided training for 'young men with a conscientious objection to being involved in military activity', but they met with a degree of resentment.[4]

WLA application processes resumed in January 1944, although in October that year it was said that all Hampshire's 'vacancies are now filled'.[5] By the end of the war, some 200,000 women and girls had been employed on full-time or part-time bases, with over 80,000 working in late 1943 and early 1944, but that number had reduced substantially by mid-1945. In that year it was thought that about one-fifth of the total farming labour force came from prisoners of war or conscientious objectors.

In addition to the large number of land girls in general agricultural settings, a separate Women's Timber Corps (WTC) was established in 1942 when imports of timber were severely constrained after Norway was occupied by German armed forces. A thousand WTC recruits were quickly engaged, becoming known as 'lumber Jills', with the number to be increased by 100 each month. By 1945, there were 6,000 lumber Jills working in England, including some in the New Forest, and another 8,000 in Scotland. The tasks undertaken included 'felling, measuring, and selecting the timber as well as sawmill work and the highly specialised job of saw sharpening'.[6] Terms of service for lumber Jills were different from those employed on farms. They worked from 7 a.m. to 4.30 p.m., rather shorter hours than their land girl counterparts, and were paid at piece rates. Average pay for 'tree fellers' was between £1/15/- and £2/6/- a week, with more paid to those exercising greater skills.

Most of the training was undertaken on-site, with some New Forest instruction in 1943 provided by members of the New Zealand Forestry Company. One Hampshire lumber Jill, Doreen Keable, born in 1923, joined the WLA in 1940 and transferred to the WTC in 1942. After a month's training she worked alongside Italian prisoners of war at sawmills at Lyndhurst and Brockenhurst, eventually being promoted to be a 'leading sawyer'. She left in 1944 when she married and moved to Canada.[7] Another Hampshire WTC member, Patricia Campbell, organised a shooting club as a recreational activity which met once a week at a number of places in the county, including the army's Barton Stacey rifle range, where contests took place against other nearby clubs.[8] The WTC was disbanded in August 1946, four years before the WLA, when all employees received an individual letter from the Queen.

A significant governmental decision, taken in May 1942 and implemented in the summer of 1943, formalised the semi-official schemes in place up to then. The harvesting need was sufficiently urgent for a designated School Release Scheme to allow boys to have up to twenty half-days away from their summer term studies providing they worked for no more than four hours a day, and that a parent or close relative gave formal approval. As in earlier years, the additional labour at key times was necessary to minimise food wastage that would arise if it proved impossible to harvest all crops. Most of the camps were for boys;

Timber Corps camp accommodation.

45,968 attended in 1944, with smaller numbers of 28,130 and 13,250 in the following two years. There were also camps for girls, the number attending peaking at 20,424 in 1943, and others for boys and girls.[9] The scheme was discontinued in 1950.

Despite the shortfall in numbers of candidates to join the WLA, some applications were controversially turned down. One case became a 'cause célèbre', receiving widespread national and local publicity. Amelia King, a 26-year-old 'coloured' girl from Stepney, east London, was employed as a 'box maker' in 1943. She was the third generation of her family to live in England, her father being a merchant navy fireman and her brother serving in the Royal Navy. In March 1943, Amelia wished to become a land girl but was discouraged from pursuing that application and advised to seek work in a local munitions factory. Difficulty in recruiting enough workers for those unpleasant environments was well known, but Amelia King completed a WLA application form, and was even fitted for the uniform she would wear when placed on a farm.

Her application was, though, refused by the Essex WLA committee because, it was claimed, farmers would be unwilling to employ her, nor would she be accepted by 'local residents with whom she would be billeted'.[10] The *News Chronicle* was the first national newspaper to be made aware of the decision, and the extensive subsequent press coverage provoked two immediate responses. Firstly, her local MP, Walter Edwards, raised the matter with Robert Hudson, Minister of Agriculture and Fisheries, in the House of Commons; and secondly, a Hampshire farmer, Alfred E. Roberts, learnt about the refusal and offered to let her join his workforce that included several land girls.

The issue became the subject of a parliamentary question in July 1943, by which time recruitment to the WLA had been suspended, thus giving another reason for the application to be turned down. Ernest Bevin, Minister of Labour in the coalition government and later Foreign Secretary in the 1945 Labour government, and Baroness Denman, Director of the WLA, both insisted that the organisation did not exercise a 'colour bar', and that the decision to decline the application was justified. Notwithstanding their standing and influence, the fuss continued. It was at last conceded that the suspension of recruitment into the WLA was a spurious and invalid ground for refusing employment as Amelia King's application had been made four months earlier.

The controversy went viral, the case being reported in newspapers all over the country, and several Hampshire farmers felt the need to 'express indignation over the case of Miss Amelia King'. Roberts commented that 'all the farmers in the district resent the injustice'.[11] He consulted his female staff, twelve of whom were WLA members, and they unanimously sympathised with Amelia King's ordeal and said they would happily work alongside her. Furthermore, supportive local people offered to provide accommodation and meals. The outcome was that in mid-October 1943 the refusal was reversed, and Amelia King joined the 100-acre Frith Farm, Wickham, 3 miles north of Fareham, run by Roberts, well-known for his production of vegetables and soft fruit. Born in 1889, Alfred Roberts had formed his agriculture and horticulture business in 1908, and although he died in 1973, the business continued to prosper. It was incorporated as A.E. Roberts (Fruit Grower & Nurseryman) Ltd in 1950, and is now known locally as Woodlea Nurseries, Winterhill, Durley, near Southampton. The company retains the name of the man who, probably unintentionally, came to national prominence with a considerate and sympathetic response to a racially motivated issue.

Amelia King worked at Frith Farm for two years, returning to London in 1945 having been discharged from the WLA on 'medical grounds'. Nothing has been discovered about her subsequent life, apart from knowing that she died at the Royal London Hospital, Whitechapel, in 1995, aged 78.[12] Her case was used at the time to highlight other barriers encountered by people of colour. In the end, in addition to Amelia's own determination, the interventions of her local MP, newspapers reporters, Alfred Roberts, Hampshire residents who provided accommodation, and other local land girls, all contributed to an acceptable outcome.

In addition to the expectations imposed on land girls, farmers had obligations to fulfil. Recognising that training establishments such as Sparsholt's Farm Institute did not have sufficient capacity to train all recruits, 'Revised Conditions' were issued in 1943. Farmers were contracted to provide four weeks of instruction on specific subjects such as milking and dairying, to limit working hours to forty-eight in the winter and fifty in the summer, and 'reduce Sunday work as much as possible'. If land girls were over 18 years of age, they were to be paid a minimum of £1/2/6d a week 'after deduction has been made to cover board and lodging'. For WLA members aged 18 and under, the minimum weekly pay was 18/-. If workers lived more than 20 miles from their work, they were entitled to a free journey home every six months with the travel cost being borne from central WLA funds.[14] At the same time, holiday entitlement was increased, but still to only one

Leaflet (1943) featuring Amelia King, issued to draw attention to racial discrimination[13]

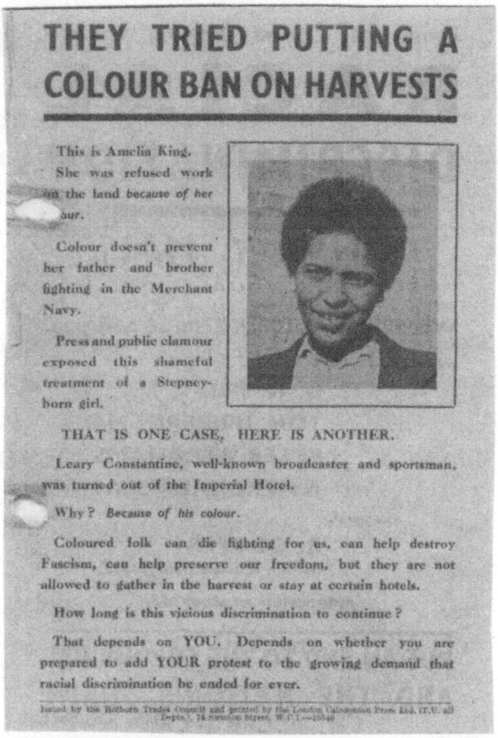

THEY TRIED PUTTING A COLOUR BAN ON HARVESTS

This is Amelia King.
She was refused work [illegible] the land *because of her* [illegible]*our.*

Colour doesn't prevent her father and brother fighting in the Merchant Navy.

Press and public clamour exposed this shameful treatment of a Stepney-born girl.

THAT IS ONE CASE, HERE IS ANOTHER.

Leary Constantine, well-known broadcaster and sportsman, was turned out of the Imperial Hotel.

Why? *Because of his colour.*

Coloured folk can die fighting for us, can help destroy Fascism, can help preserve our freedom, but they are not allowed to gather in the harvest or stay at certain hotels.

How long is this vicious discrimination to continue?

That depends on YOU. Depends on whether you are prepared to add YOUR protest to the growing demand that racial discrimination be ended for ever.

Issued by the Holborn Trades Council and printed by the London Caledonian Press Ltd. (T.U. all Depts.), 74 Swinton Street, W.C.1.—15546

Land girls at Frith Farm, Wickham, including Amelia King (circa 1944). (Wickham History Society)

week per annum. In addition, land girls had just one day off each week, and were expected to be granted one free weekend in four. Farmers had to ensure that training began on a Monday, and in exchange for the teaching and employment of recruits, they were paid £1 per week.[15]

In 1944, the NFU told the government that around 100,000 former male land-based workers were likely to return at the end of hostilities and would expect to be offered their jobs back. In recognition of the need for their retraining, it was no coincidence that additional land-based training institutions were established in the post-war years to provide for those armed forces members who wished to resume farming employment.[16] In September that year, the Ministry of Agriculture announced that a training scheme was under active consideration that would 'provide practical training in agriculture and horticulture for men and women released from the uniformed services'.[17] Sparsholt Farm Institute's governing body had, regrettably, to say that the relative inaccessibility of the campus via public transport would mean that only injured military personnel who were mobile could attend retraining there.

A separate scheme was introduced for women and girls who had worked in agricultural, office and factory settings to train as school-teachers.[18] Yet another government initiative, at its cost, was the offer of specialist instruction for WLA members if their 'further education had been interrupted or had prevented courses of higher education'.[19] Many, though, wished to stay with the outdoor life; 'often one hears a Land Girl say she will not go back to the counter, office or factory'.[20]

Because there was the distinct possibility that many land girls might be expected, or forced, to lose the occupation they had become accustomed to when the war ended, a WLA Benevolent Fund had been set up in July 1942. One of the key sponsors was Clementine Ogilvy Spencer-Churchill, wife of the prime minister. She was known for 'her deep commitment to humanitarian causes and her dedication to addressing moral concerns',[21] and urged support for the fund 'to relieve cases of hardship and, after the War, to enable women to become students at agricultural colleges where they will be trained for farming life in Britain or for work in the Dominions'.[22]

Among other benefits, the fund would cover tuition costs to prepare members for 'civilian jobs where free training was not available', as well as providing 'grants towards the expenses of illness and convalescence'.[23] In 1944, a 'Homecraft Training Centre' was established for land girls 'about to leave the WLA and get married'[24] to have a month's residential training, and three 'Rest-break Houses' were opened at Torquay, Llandudno and Edinburgh. The fund aimed to raise £50,000 by the end of 1943 and £100,000 by the end of 1944. In May 1943, it was reported that £25,318 had been contributed,[25] a figure that grew to £36,000 five months later, no doubt helped by donations following a Sunday morning BBC 'Week's Good Cause' appeal. A year later, £71,836 had been donated, including £10,000 from a Treasury payment, and 854 grants had been provided to successful land girl applicants.[26]

The proceeds of many organised occasions in Hampshire were donated to the Benevolent Fund. A dance took place at Titchfield in May 1943, and at New Milton dances became regular events in the summer months. Throughout 1944, dances and whist drives were held in many places, with local newspapers in 1945 frequently noting activities at, among other places, Petersfield, Durley, West Dean, Havant, Emsworth and Rowland Castle. Among more unusual events, a play written and produced by a WLA member was well received by an appreciative audience at Liphook.

While a few farmers were reluctant to employ women and girls until necessity dictated otherwise, expressions of gratitude were constantly being received. An edition of *The Land Girl* in October 1942 reported that, 'during the last month the office has received more letters from farmers praising the girls than ever before.'[27] A letter to a local newspaper in February 1944 said: 'What farmers would do without the help of the Women's Land Army at the present time is hard to say, for time after time they have helped farms short of labour, working together in gangs.'[28] The value of WLA service is epitomised by 'a story from Hampshire of a farmer taken away to hospital, leaving no one but his two land-girls to run his 150-acre farm'.[29] They looked after the farm on their own for five weeks, starting each day at 5.30 a.m. Another fulsome appreciation was made by E. Walford Lloyd, a frequent Hampshire local newspaper contributor on agriculture matters, who wrote that, 'members of the WLA have performed yeoman service in all kinds of weathers, and at all types of farm work, and the country owes them a greater debt of gratitude than is, perhaps, generally realised.'[30] One way of formally acknowledging the contributions of land girls was the presentation to them of red 'armlets' after four years of continuous service.

Lady Gertrude Denman, the inspirational Honorary Director of the WLA, who saw at first hand the achievements of land girls, claimed with justification that they have 'carried on arduous and trying work on the land, often at serious personal risk'.[31] A frequently quoted early saying from her was prophetic. In 1939, as the war was just beginning, she said, 'The land army fights in the fields. It is in the fields of Britain that the most critical battle of the present war may well be fought and won.'[32] Cases of particular merit were publicised. One Hampshire land girl, Thelma Hanan, had joined the WLA straight from school in 1942, and in January 1945 was working on a farm at Mottisfont. Although having 'never handled a plough or any other farming implement before',[33] she outpointed eight men to win a county-wide tractor ploughing competition. Thelma Hanan was a talented young lady; she was awarded first prize in a national competition to design an advertising poster for the WLA Benevolent Fund in 1943, and when she gave up being a land girl, she became a very well-regarded student of the County School of Art at Worthing.

Pauline Woolmer White played a pivotal role in dealing with the challenges and successes of the WLA. She had been appointed 'chairman' of Hampshire's WLA committee in July 1942, a task that took up a great deal of time and energy. It was because of the increased WLA commitment that she resigned as honorary secretary of the Havant branch of the Conservative Association in June 1943. Woolmer White's huge contributions were acknowledged in May 1945 when she received a Gold Certificate from the Ministry of Agriculture, the wording saying: 'The task of British agriculture, an arduous, indeed a vital one, was to keep the nation fed. With your help it has been done.'[34] Her work continued well after the war ended, organising many rally and recruitment parades, including one in Southampton in May 1946, and chairing numerous meetings with Hampshire County and national officials. After dedicated service to the WLA during both world wars, Pauline Woolmer White died at her home in Rowland Castle in 1980, aged 88.

Vacancies for land girls to work in Hampshire reappeared in June 1945, and the person directly responsible for placing them on farms was Olive Catherine Huskisson. She was born in 1898, the daughter of Colonel William Huskisson, came to Hampshire soon after the war began, and was the WLA county secretary throughout the six war years. As just one example, she wrote to Mr P. Denham of Stapleford Farm, Durley, in 1945 to remind him that, 'your name has been on our books for a very long time as needing a girl. I have not been able to fill your vacancy before owing to a shortage of girls.'[35] A year later, though, the recruitment position had eased, and Denham responded to another letter to say that he still needed help. A suitable girl was found for him; 'Miss Olive Slade is eighteen years of age, has had an elementary education, and seems a nice, quiet type.'[36] A month later, Denham reported that she was 'getting on so well', and he was authorised to place her 'on a Government Training Basis as from Monday July 1st'. [37] It was expected that Denham himself would provide the training.

As the end of the war approached, farmers were 'growing nervous that many members of the WLA will take advantage of the scheme for releasing them from their work'.[38] Recognising the potential shortfall, the Ministry of Agriculture appealed to land girls to stay on for another year. It turned out to be an entirely appropriate message, as in parts of Hampshire very few who left farms to serve in the military took up their previous employment. Long-serving Hampshire county councillor R.T. Moore expressed disquiet that in his locality around Andover 'only one of 14 men who left agricultural work returned'[39] to farming after the war. In some cases, men chose a different employment path, and in others serious injuries prevented the ability to undertake physical work.

In October 1945, the WLA's chief administration officer sent a letter to between 700 and 800 land girls who 'will qualify for their six-year armlets'. They were to be distributed by the Queen at a special Christmas party at the Mansion House, London, in December. Hampshire land girls who would have served for six continuous years to December 1945 were urged to accept the invitation, and would be taken to London by a specially chartered bus.[40]

A clear dichotomy for the government was that it could not anticipate whether large numbers of former agricultural workers would return to their jobs and displace women and girls, or, as was the case around Andover, men chose or were forced to seek alternative employment. This dilemma was exemplified by the introduction of 'gratuity' and 'business grants' schemes for most wartime occupations undertaken by women. They were introduced in the expectation that there would need to be encouragement for women and girls to leave their wartime jobs when men returned. To the intense dissatisfaction of Lady Denman, the schemes did not, though, apply to WLA members, and she resigned in protest in February 1945, saying that, 'it does seem hard that they should not be eligible for a gratuity.'[41]

The situation was not helped by a speech from John R. Lambley, national organiser of the National Union of Agricultural Workers, who told a rally at Andover that he knew 'they [land girls] have a grievance against the Government with regard to their gratuities',[42] but they should accept the decision. Lambley, born in December 1892, became a long-serving trade union official, a local authority councillor, and an unsuccessful Labour candidate in at least two general elections in 1932 and 1951. His support for workers in agricultural settings remained solely focused on male labourers and did not extend to land girls.

Despite the Ministry of Agriculture announcing in February 1945 that a scheme for land girls 'is under separate and sympathetic consideration',[43] and three months later saying that specialist higher education training would be made available so that WLA members could apply for 'posts in advisory, instructional and research services',[44] the issue did not subside. As a modest concession, land girls who had served for six months were to be allowed to 'retain a great coat, one pair of shoes and a shirt', but a Conservative MP complained that the proposals were 'totally inadequate' and 'mean and niggardly'.[45] A year later, in April 1946, a resolution was passed by a Hampshire Women's Institute branch, recording that land girls 'should receive the same gratuities and benefits as accorded to members of other women's services'.[46]

# 11

# Continuing Role for Women's Land Army After 1945

The ending of the war in Europe prompted much celebration. At 3 p.m. on VE Day, 8 May 1945, the prime minister, Winston Churchill, made a radio broadcast to the nation, and then attended a service at St Margaret's Church, Westminster, 'to give humble and reverent thanks to Almighty God for our deliverance from the threat of German domination'.[1] In Hampshire there were many events marking the German surrender. In Aldershot, publicans extended their drinking hours, a Canadian pipe band played through the town, bonfires were lit, and between 8,000 and 10,000 people gathered in Aldershot's recreation ground.[2] The main official Winchester celebration was held on 15 August when the cathedral bells were rung, and a service was held at 12 noon, attended by nearly 1,000 people.[3] At Southampton, over 500 members of the WLA took part in a 'Victory and Recruitment Parade'.

Once the euphoria surrounding the end of hostilities had abated, attention focused on the government's continued determination to emphasise the need to maximise home-grown food production to reduce dependence on imports. As only a quarter of Hampshire's WLA members were 'taking their release',[4] there were still about 800 land girls working in the county. One area of potential greater employment for women was promoted by the vice chairman of Hampshire's NFU, who stressed opportunities in horticultural businesses, saying that 'this side of the industry would develop out of all knowledge'.[5] However, the combination of land girls leaving farm-based jobs, some to undertake further education studies, and fewer men than expected taking up their previous jobs, meant,

Land girls driving tractors at a Rally, Southampton, 1946.

once again, that a Hampshire recruitment campaign was launched. One advertisement proclaimed, '"FOOD COMES FIRST", the war is over, but the Battle for Food goes on'.[6] A year later, in May 1947, it was again widely recognised that Hampshire had been 'one of the leading counties for the employment of members of the WLA on farms and market gardens, and girls are still enrolling to take their part in the Battle for Bread'.[7]

The raising of the school leaving age to 15 in 1947, and the departure from British shores of former prisoners of war, resulted, yet again, in a shortage of workers on farms. A 'Ferguson Tractors & Implements' advertisement in 1948 noted that the government required a 20 per cent increase in home food production, and a leading article in a local newspaper was headed 'Exhortation to Land Girls' 'We Cannot Let Up'. More female volunteers were soon ready, and although they were 'untrained in farm work they are proving to be keen and once trained they are a valuable asset'.[8] The need was also emphasised by Tom Williams, Minister for Agriculture, who said that the 'rebuilding of the WLA which did such splendid service during the war years'[9] was again necessary.

At a rally of Hampshire land girls in May 1948, Frank Miles, JP, Mayor of Portsmouth, and an influential Hampshire farmer, noted that 200 more recruits were needed for Hampshire, and that there was 'no better job for girls than to take to the land and enjoy the healthy fresh air and exercise'. If that was not a clear enough exhortation, the vice chairman of Hampshire's County Executive Committee asserted on the same occasion that 'during the war the Land Army was in the fourth line of defence – Today it was the first line of Defence.' On the same occasion, Pauline Woolmer White and Catherine Huskisson, respectively Hampshire's WLA committee 'chairman' and secretary, were singled out for 'the wonderful service they had given to the organisation'.[10] That was an entirely appropriate commendation, as in focusing on the intensively practical work of land girls, it was important not to overlook the huge commitment of Hampshire volunteers in other capacities.

Despite continuing appeals for more land-based workers, in February 1948 Woolmer White and Huskisson jointly wrote two letters to WLA members that appeared to undermine the value of the contributions given by so many people. The first told them that after 1 June 1948 'all voluntary work will cease', and the second, a few days later, announced that 'War Ag' committees were, under the terms of the 1947 Agriculture Act, to be superseded by County Agricultural Executive Committees.[11] The WLA was not the only body confused by the apparent contradiction and mixed messages. Members of Parliament regularly questioned government ministers about the logic of reducing the need for WLA member volunteers while food rationing remained in place, and shortages of labour on farms were apparent.

A year before the war ended, Sparsholt's Farm Institute had reverted to its pre-war curriculum while accepting some females to undertake a general agricultural course that equipped them to join the WLA. One 17-year-old student who came to the institute for a year in 1946, after acquiring useful skills working at the Chatsworth estate in Derbyshire, was Elizabeth Cheal, later Mrs Bridges. The course involved a wide variety of lessons and practical work on a weekly rotation basis. Over a two-week period, she was instructed on dairy, horticulture and poultry matters. Cows had to be fetched from fields, milked, and returned, the horticultural work was mainly in greenhouses, but she also 'learnt to mow the lawns'. Poultry work included careful recording of egg laying performances, and 'killing, plucking and trussing chickens'.[12]

Elizabeth's first land girl job after her successful year at Sparsholt was on a 50-acre local farm where 'she had two cows to milk, a pig to raise for meat, chickens to look after'. She then worked on the Craig Harvey family Lainston Estate on the edge of Sparsholt village where, in addition to milking and butter-making, Elizabeth had charge of 700 turkeys reared for the Christmas trade. A painful experience for her was an outbreak of foot-and-mouth disease in 1948 that led to the digging of large pit, and she 'was given the job of walking each animal to the edge of the pit where the vet shot them to fall into the pit'. She also helped with haymaking, and among the more unusual tasks were 'beating the undergrowth to disturb' pheasants that were then shot, and 'ferreting' to force rabbits to exit their holes to be killed by the farmer's local friends. Elizabeth continued to work on farms in Hampshire and East Sussex, being one of the large numbers of land girls who continued farm work after demobilisation of the WLA in November 1950. She recorded that the Young Farmers' Club was regarded as 'the farmers' marriage bureau', and it was where she met her future husband in 1950, married him in 1951, and continued to work as a farm secretary.[13]

To attract additional workers, wages rates had been rising significantly since 1943. The weekly rate in 1944 was £2/17/6d, although that was still much lower than the amounts paid to women in other wartime employment. It was increased again in July 1946, when the weekly wage was to be £3 for women aged 21 and over, £2/12/6d for those between 18 and 21, and £2/7/- for girls between 17 and 18, 'abated' for the first two months of employment. The continuing need for land girls was prompted by the intention to reduce food imports, with the aim, eventually, to remove the necessity to ration food. That was not fully achieved until 1954.

Despite regular appeals to existing land girls to remain on farms and to attract others to come forward, national numbers fell quickly once the war ended. From a WLA membership peak of 87,000 in 1943, it reduced to 47,861 in 1944, and to 43,124 in 1945. The rate of reduction then accelerated: to 11,210 in 1949 and to 6,824 when the WLA was formally disbanded on 30 November 1950.[14] On departure, each land girl was issued with a 'Release Certificate' showing her starting and finishing dates.

The WLA Benevolent Fund, established in 1942, continued to attract financial contributions when the war was over. At the Brockenhurst Horticultural Show in 1947, produce was sold for the benefit of former land girls in need. In July, a target was set to produce another £1,000 by the end of the year, to achieve an overall Hampshire total of £10,000. Impressively, over five years nearly 1,000 land girls had been directly helped, and other monies were used 'towards the upkeep of the Rest Break Houses, Homecraft Training Centres, Convalescence Homes etc.'.[15]

To the dismay of many, the imminent disbandment of the WLA had become apparent during 1949, and in August that year the closure of hostels began apace. County committees were instructed to reduce labour

WOMEN'S LAND ARMY
WOMEN'S LAND ARMY (ENGLAND & WALES).
RELEASE CERTIFICATE.
The Women's Land Army for England and Wales acknowledges with appreciation the services given by
Miss Jeanne Mason.
who has been an enrolled member for the period from
31st. March 1943 to 27th. August 1947.
and has this day been granted a willing release.
Date 5th. August 1947.
WOMEN'S LAND ARMY.

'Release Certificate' for Jeanne Mason, 5 August 1947.

forces in advance of the formal demobilisation. Belatedly, a month later, the Ministry of Agriculture issued a low-key farewell circular message of thanks to WLA members, telling them that the 'jobs [were] often more arduous and less well rewarded than that undertaken by the women who went into factories'.[16] The final official parade to commemorate the work of the WLA was held on 21 October 1950. It began with a march to Buckingham Palace, where the Queen presented long-service medals to 800 land girls, and in an address to them she said: 'The story of the Land Army has been one of a great response ... in the nation's hour of need ... By their hard work and patient endurance they earned a noble share in the immense effort which carried our country to victory.'[17] The closing comment in *The Land Girl* was that WLA members 'had obeyed the call of duty in the nation's hour of great peril and need, and the nation owed them an everlasting debt'.[18]

In early 1950, statistics relating to the increase in food production for the previous year were published which, to an extent, quantified the contributions that land girls continued to make. A.W. Garrett, a regular Hampshire reporter on farming matters, produced an extensive article on post-war progress: milk yields and cow herd sizes had improved to a level that enabled rationing on milk-related products to be removed despite consumption being 50 per cent higher than pre-war levels; poultry numbers had increased by 6 million to 39.69 million over the previous six months; sheep flocks contained 9 million animals, having recovered from a sharp reduction three years earlier; there were 2.5 million pigs, a rise of 150,000 in a year; and 280,000 more acres of wheat had been harvested than in 1948. Those creditable performances were achieved despite falling numbers of farm workers from 716,000 in 1948 to 691,600 in 1949. The workforce decline since the end of the war was caused by the return of male labourers being insufficient to offset fewer casual and full-time women workers, and the repatriation of most of the remaining prisoners of war. Despite those reductions, the overall number was still 25,000 higher than when the war began in 1939.[19]

Marking the demobilisation of Hampshire's WLA, many officials and land girls were present at a Thanksgiving Service at Winchester Cathedral, led by Right Rev. Mervyn Haigh, Bishop of Winchester, on Saturday, 14 October 1950. His remarks to the congregation stated that the whole nation was 'conscious of the great debt we owe to those who, in spite of every difficulty, worked so heroically … to increase our food supplies'. As a moving final gesture, 'students of the County Farm Institute at Sparsholt escorted a trolley down the aisle which bore horticultural and agricultural produce.'[20] During the service, the 'Hymn of the Hampshire Country-side',[21] specially written for the occasion by Dr E.G. Selwyn, Dean of Winchester Cathedral, and Rev. J.P. Boden, the cathedral's precentor, was sung. The hymn was subsequently included in harvest festival services in parish churches around the county: Odiham in 1953, Sway in 1954 and in more recent years at St Michael and All Angels, Highclere. It was also included in an assembly at Andover Grammar School in 1968.

Thus came the end of the WLA organisation that had successfully served the nation in two hugely important respects. Land girls became able substitutes for the hundreds of thousands of men who served in the war and, secondly, they contributed to a significant rise in the volumes of home-produced food, so minimising the nation's reliance on imports. The WLA's worth to the nation did not end with the war, as the target of increasing food production still further remained central to government policy. The closure of the WLA was still regretted a year later when, in 1951, a parliamentary resolution was debated: 'This house … is concerned that having disbanded the Women's Land Army, the Government proposes still further to deplete the labour force by a call up of agricultural workers.'[22] Statistically, that assertion was confirmed: between June 1951 and June 1955, the number of farm workers in this country fell from 554,000 to 480,000.

In September 1950, Hampshire newspapers included letters submitted to editors seeking to establish if there was likely to be sufficient demand to form Old Girls' Associations for former WLA members. A Hampshire association, with the formal title 'ex-Women's Land Army (Hampshire branch)', was set up at the end of 1950 with the object 'to maintain a spirit of comradeship amongst those who have been connected with the WLA'. By May 1951, the association's committee included Mrs Norah Hull, Westridge Cottage, Highclere, as 'chairman', and Mrs Martha Madeley, 'Westfield', Bereweeke Road, Winchester, as secretary. Among committee members was, almost inevitably, Pauline Woolmer White, who continued her very long association with the WLA. There were to be two meetings and two news bulletins, each year.

Several branches of the association were formed, newsletters were periodically issued, and annual meetings were held in Winchester, but in March 1968 newspaper reports announced that it was to be closed down. At the invitation of E. Kenneth Griffiths, principal of what was by then called the Hampshire College of Agriculture, the final event comprising a tea, a farewell speech, and a tour of the Sparsholt campus was held on 27 April 1968. At its peak, the association had 2,000 members, but that had dwindled to just twenty-five. The balance of funds in the association, £15/11/9d, was given to the Benevolent Fund, whose 'chief work is to help in sickness and … widows with children'.[23] At the final meeting it was said that Berkshire was then the only English county to have a continuing association.

Offers to help former land girls came, too, from Hampshire branches of the Women's Institute (WI) when, in March 1951, the WI took over from the Women's Royal Voluntary Service the responsibility to provide any necessary support. It was thought that 221 ex-members of the WLA were still employed in the county. A letter from Diane Darling, Hampshire's WI Secretary, in April 1951, asked local branches, of which there were 103, to identify a person to act as a 'friendly link with ex-members of WLA who are still working in Hampshire', and to be a 'friend in need'.[24] Among responses, one came from the Liss WI group saying that they could 'find you a motherly person … who would willingly cope with lonely or afflicted land girls'.[25] Several other branches, though, reported that the identified land girls had either left the county, were living with relatives, or were no longer involved in land-based work.

In 1965, twenty years after the end of the war, Pauline Woolmer White asked if the Hampshire branch of the NFU would 'house the banner of the Hampshire branch of the Women's Land Army'. It had been made in September 1943 by the Royal School of Needlework at a total cost of £33/1/6d.[26] The NFU's General Purposes Committee agreed, and W.J. Keenleyside, county secretary, replied that the NFU would be 'only too pleased to have the Women's Land Army banner in our County Office here as a mark of respect and appreciation for the work of the Women's Land Army during the crucial war years'.[27]

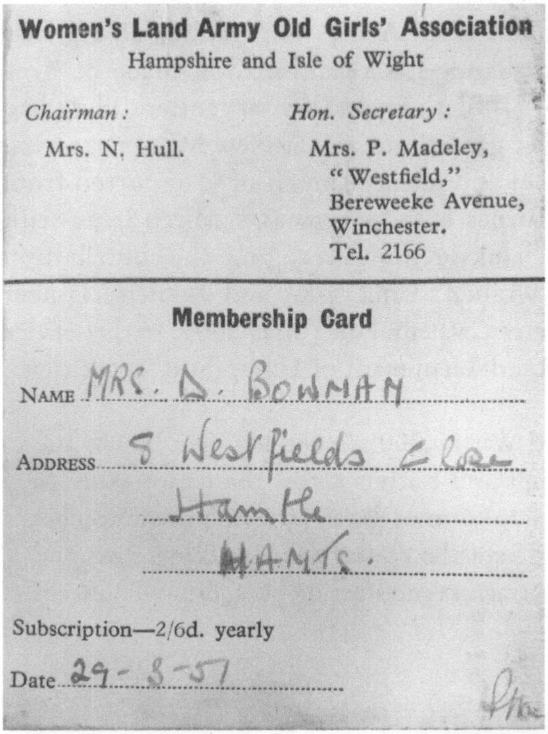

**Women's Land Army Old Girls' Association**
Hampshire and Isle of Wight

*Chairman :* Mrs. N. Hull.

*Hon. Secretary :* Mrs. P. Madeley, "Westfield," Bereweeke Avenue, Winchester. Tel. 2166

**Membership Card**

NAME MRS. D. BOWMAN

ADDRESS 8 Westfields Close
Hamble
HANTS.

Subscription—2/6d. yearly

Date 29-3-51

Membership Card, Women's Land Army Old Girls Association, Hampshire and Isle of Wight; Mrs D. Bowman, 29 March 1951. (HRO ref; 50M90/6)

Final Reunion of Women's Land Army Old Girls' Association, Hampshire and Isle of Wight, 27 April 1968.

Although the ex-Women's Land Army Association (Hampshire Branch) had long been disbanded, a reunion took place of nine former land girls in 1996, all of them in their seventies. They had worked together at a market garden nursery at New Milton growing large quantities of tomatoes and lettuce, much of it exported from Southampton to armed forces based overseas.[28] Much later still, 'A Hampshire Service of Thanksgiving to recognise the contribution made by members of The Women's Land Army and Women's Timber Corps' was held in Winchester Cathedral on 7 May 2009. In the service programme, Mary Fagan, Lord-Lieutenant of Hampshire, wrote that:

> During the Second World War 80,000 women left their homes and families to live in lodgings and hostels across the countryside to work on farms. Wearing a uniform of green jerseys, brown breeches and brown felt hats, they kept the country fed, milking cows and mucking-out pigs, driving tractors and steering ploughs, sowing seeds and harvesting crops.[29]

Programme of the 'Hampshire Service of Thanksgiving to recognise the contribution made by members of the Women's Land Army and Women's Timber Corps', 7 May 2009.

# 12

# Conclusion

Official WLA membership numbers of land girls working in every British county up to 31 December 1943 were published in 1944. Hampshire newspapers reported rapid local growth from 200 in November 1939, to 350 in mid-1940, and 600 in June 1941. Included in the national figures, Hampshire, including the Isle of Wight, recorded 1,039 at December 1941, increasing to 2,091 and 2,611 by the end of 1943.[1] Hampshire numbers probably fell to around 1,500 by early 1946 and to about 300 by the time the WLA was formally demobilised in November 1950.

This book's Preface refers to claims that work carried out on farms by land girls was regarded as a 'Cinderella' operation, less appreciated by the authorities than those employed in other wartime occupations. One writer complained that: 'Official recognition of their role has been woefully late in coming. When the Women's Land Army was disbanded in 1950 the members were shabbily treated, receiving neither medals nor gratuities, and being required to return most of their uniforms.'[2] Support for that view comes from knowing that not until 2000 were land girls invited to march past the Cenotaph on Remembrance Day, and it was only in January 2008 that surviving members of the WLA, estimated to number around 20,000, could obtain commemorative badges. As *The Independent* put it:

> Dressed in a scratchy uniform of brown woollen breeches, a green jumper and a shirt and tie, they were the women whose back-breaking labours in milking parlours, lumber yards and on muddy fields helped to ensure that Britain did not starve during the Second World War. While a grateful nation later saluted its fighting forces, the 80,000

> members of the Women's Land Army (WLA) received scant official recognition. The government only begrudgingly paid them a £150 resettlement allowance after the Queen made clear her support for their cause.[3]

And it took another six years to October 2014 before a statue was unveiled at the National Arboretum, Alrewas, Staffordshire. The bronze memorial, standing on a rectangular white sandstone plinth, shows members of the Women's Land Army and the Timber Corps holding examples of the tools used in their work. It was formally unveiled by HRH The Countess of Wessex in the presence of approximately 400 former WLA members, their families and friends. The wording records that 'During the first and second world wars over 240,000 land girls and lumber jills provided food and timber for the war efforts. On behalf of our nation, we extend our thanks and appreciation for the commitment and endeavour shown by these young women.'

WLA and Women's Timber Corps Memorial. (Egghead06, CC BY-SA 4.0, Wikimedia Commons)

Careful study of material relevant to Hampshire provides countless examples of the value and commitment given by thousands of women and girls to the county's farmers. The fact that rationing limited wartime availability of most food products, and Britain's population suffered hardships, does not disguise recognition that, nationally, huge numbers of women and girls ensured that even more austere Second World War restrictions did not need to be imposed. While politicians and local authorities created, understandably, a decision-making hierarchy, the role of WLA members in agricultural settings can be summarised by a comment from a different context: they served 'with such distinction that grounds for opposition grew ever harder to justify'.[4] Leaving others to deal with strategic, leadership and management responsibilities, land girls, in intensely physical working environments, literally, as well as metaphorically, kept their proverbial 'heads down', to deliver outstanding contributions to feeding the nation in two world wars. The universally used saying 'We Will Remember Them' must apply just as much to the women and girls of the WLA as it does to those who were directly involved in armed conflict abroad.

# Appendices

## Appendix A: Profile of a Land Girl – Gwendoline (Gwen) Raggett (née Place) MBE

Of the hundreds of thousands of land girls who gave unstinting service to the country during two twentieth-century world wars, it is unlikely that anyone exceeded the commitment of Gwen Raggett. In a conversation with her in December 2023, she was able, at the age of 97, to recall personal events that gave an indication of the depth and breadth of the tasks she was expected to undertake as a member of the WLA.[1]

Gwendoline Place, born in Bournemouth on 29 June 1926, was a clever girl who won a scholarship to continue her education, but her parents were unable to afford the financial cost of further schooling. Gwen left, aged 14, and found work locally as a cinema cashier, where her manager considered her to be the only honest one he had ever employed. He was, not surprisingly, 'furious' when Gwen told him she would be resigning to join the WLA.

Gwen's father 'forbade me to join the armed forces', so she answered the increasingly desperate call for girls to help the war effort in the United Kingdom. She visited the local Labour Exchange and, in marked contrast to the experience of most WLA candidates, Gwen submitted herself to a perfunctory interview undertaken at the home of an official before being accepted. She expressed a preference to join the Women's Timber Corps, many members of which were employed in the New Forest, but she was guided to apply for the main agricultural section of the WLA. So it was that on 12 August 1943, aged 17 years and 2 months, she and nine other girls from Hampshire south coast cities and towns travelled together to become the first residents of Redenham House, a large mansion taken over as a WLA hostel, 5 miles east of Andover, close to the Wiltshire border.

Although there was a well-established land-based training institution at Sparsholt, other training centres around the county, and many 'approved' farms, most land girls, including Gwen, simply learnt 'on the job'. Given the diverse, technically, and physically challenging range of duties they were expected to undertake over a farming year, that was a stiff task, and the guidance provided was rudimentary. As an example, thatching was an important skilled activity, but these land girls were expected to undertake the job after being told just once what they had to do. The physicality of the work sometimes took its toll on them. There was an occasion when Gwen 'had been working hard in the field all day and hurt her back … she was in so much pain, she had to crawl on her hands and knees all the way up the driveway to the House',[2] a distance of well over ½ mile.

Remarkably, and possibly before her 18th birthday, Gwen was already driving the 3-tonne lorry that was used to transport Redenham land girls to the various farms where they were assigned. In most circumstances, driving tests for cars and lorries were suspended during the war years, but Gwen took one in Winchester on a particularly busy market day. She remembers the examiner standing on the running board of the lorry to check that its wheels did not touch the kerb or, worse, mount the pavement! Despite having just two lessons, Gwen was successful and for the remainder of her time with the WLA she took on the duty of transporting about ten girls, precariously seated in two rows on the back of the lorry, to their allocated farms.

There was a hierarchical structure to the WLA, and Gwen was soon promoted to 'gang leader', not a universally popular role as she had to ensure the girls were out of their bunks and ready to start the day's duties on time. She delivered girls to the assigned farms and collected them at the end of the working day. And then she had to take the lorry's rotor arm off and empty the water tank. Practical experience of farming needs and vehicle maintenance were not the totality of Gwen's expertise. As the war continued, proficiency examinations were introduced, and Gwen passed a comprehensive one relating to 'market garden and field work' in January 1945. She still has the 'Mark Sheet' showing the allocation of the marks. A wide variety of practical topics were tested: 'load a wagon with sheaves of hay or straw'; 'riddle potatoes in a hand riddle'; and 'from the plants provided plant out two rows at a suitable distance apart', were three – 'Special marks being awarded for speed'. Furthermore, there was an 'oral' part to the examination when five subjects were tested, including knowledge of the rotation of crops, common diseases, and reasons for crop failures. There were opportunities for recreational activities and Gwen took a leading part in a play put on by Redenham's residents, and at a later reunion was a member of the women's cricket team that played a match against local farmers.

With a ready smile and a twinkle in her eye, Gwen brings to mind two confessed misdemeanours. As was normal, smoking in bedrooms and dormitories was strictly forbidden, but Gwen and others did not always comply with the instruction, and on one occasion the strict but fair-minded matron, Moyra Drake-Brockman, knocked on the dormitory door, suspecting that smoking was taking place. The land girls quickly extinguished their cigarettes and nothing more was said. The more serious incident followed Gwen's decision to remove part of her uniform while thatching in hot weather. The farmer on whose farm she was working took a photograph, which was published in a local newspaper. It was brought to the attention of WLA officials, and one of them thought the offence warranted travelling from Bournemouth to Redenham House, not the most straightforward of journeys, to issue a severe reprimand! Gwen was not, though, the only land girl to consider that the standard uniform WLA members were expected to wear was unsuitable.

Gwen remembers the events surrounding the outbreak of the fire at the top of Redenham House on a Saturday in September 1946. She was one of a small number of land girls resident over that weekend, and was the one who first alerted the fire brigade. Fire engines appeared from different parts of Hampshire and farther afield, and the fire was extinguished reasonably promptly, although most of the roof was destroyed and there was extensive water damage to the lower floors. Land girls were relocated to another hostel nearby.

The Redenham estate was sold by auction in September 1948 and the WLA gave up accommodating land girls there soon afterwards. Over the course of the war, many new recruits were sent to hostels and farms a long way from their homes – one group of ten girls arrived at Redenham

House from Walsall, Staffordshire – but Gwen was transferred to hostels at Burley, Holmsley and Beaulieu, all in the south of the county and closer to her Bournemouth family home.

After Gwen married and left the WLA in 1949, she gave her time and expertise for the benefit of several voluntary organisations. Probably the most significant started in 1964, when she began a regular van-driving weekly commitment with the Women's Voluntary Service for Civil Defence, that later became the WRVS. She delivered 'Meals on Wheels', library books for those with mobility problems, and helped at baby clinics. Gwen was later appointed to organise the book rounds and the volunteers, only giving up the responsibilities when, in her early nineties, Covid put a stop to such activities. She also helped to establish the Bournemouth Stroke Club, and participated in the setting up of a camp in 1979 for over 500 Vietnam refugees at a former RAF

Gwen Raggett, 1926, aged 17.
(Copy supplied by GR)

Land girls, and officials, in front of the main entrance to Redenham House, 1947. Gwen is seated on the ground, second in from the right. (Copy supplied by GR)

base at Sopley. Her outstanding voluntary service was justly recognised with the award of an MBE in 2005.

Widowed in January 2018 when Maurice, a childhood sweetheart and husband for sixty-eight years, died, Gwen, now physically somewhat frail, retains an amazingly agile mind which can readily recall many events. She retains an innate affection for the girls with whom she shared accommodation and a working environment, remembering the names of many. Having lived in the Bournemouth area for very many years, Gwen is well-known locally, and is surrounded by a supportive, caring family of two sons, their wives, three grandchildren and five great-grandchildren. The huge volume of retained personal memorabilia is being arranged by a family member, and is an everlasting and enduring testament to her life of service. In a world that often feels increasingly selfish and individualistic, Gwen Raggett, MBE, epitomises people whose largely unsung and unpaid community service is a beacon and an example to us all.[3]

## Appendix B: Hymn of the Hampshire Countryside

Praise we the Lord, the great Author of Nature,
Praise we the Maker of upland and plain;
Praise we the Spirit through whom every creature
Gathers its life and renews it again.

Once did the Son of God (mighty the wonder)
Walk this earth's dusty paths, tread on its loam;
Once did he look on the harvest, and ponder;
'Where is the labour to fetch it all home?'

Lord, we would serve thee and turn to thy glory
All our best efforts of mind and of hand;
Lord, we would see the old heavenly story
Made flesh again in the soil of our land.

Are not the waters of the Test and of Avon
Meet for thy christening as Jordan's of old?
May not our downs, with thy foot-prints engraven,
Like Judah's mountains thy cradle enfold?

Oft in the starry night waking or sleeping
On the hard stones thou reclindest thine head:
Wilt thou not rest where our Forest is heaping
Leaves for thy pillow and ling for thy bed?

Once for the gardener did Mary mistake thee
In the grey mists of the first Easter Day:
Lord, we have gardens, and fain would we make the
Master of all their resplendent array.

See where his flock the young shepherd is guiding
Hard by the track on Old Winchester Hill:
See where 'mid Alton's shy slopes lie in hiding
Kilns where the hops their soft odours distil.

Jesus, our Saviour, in mercy be near us:
Shepherd and Sower and reaper art thou:
Pardon our sins, let thy charity cheer us;
Hallow the harvest we bring to thee now.

Written in 1950 by Dr Edward Gordon Selwyn (1885–1959), and Rev. John Posnett Boden (1894–1985), respectively dean and precentor of Winchester Cathedral. It was sung to the tune 'Epiphany'.

## Appendix C: Two Poems Written by Isabella D.S. Waddell in 1941, Aged 22

**'Women's Land Army'**

We women of this empire
Heard our country's call
And so we joined the Land Army
And backs now to the wall

Now twenty thousand strong are we
From John O'Groats to Lands End
We'll till and sow our good old earth
Until this war does end

And victory then ours will be
We'll beat those rotten huns
And when that happy day is here
We know our job is done

But girls before I finish this
If at a loss [of] what to do
Join the Women's Land Army
And help to see it through

**[Untitled]**

I'm as happy as can be
On my tractor all day long
Just the good old earth and me
And in my heart a song

The birds all sing around me
The leaves are turning brown
And in another week or two
I'll see them tumble down

As down to earth they tumble
All playing with the wind
The poor old trees are left quite bare
Until the early Spring

Isabella D.S. Waddell in her Women's Land Army uniform.

## Appendix D: Women's Land Army Uniform

The normal issue in mid-1944 was:

> 3 green jerseys, 2 pairs of breeches, 2 overall coats, 2 pairs dungarees, 6 pairs of stockings, 3 shirts, 1 pair of ankle socks, 1 pair of shoes, 1 pair of gumboots or boots with leggings, 1 hat, 1 overcoat with shoulder titles, 1 oilskin or mackintosh, 2 towels, an oilskin sou'-wester, a green armlet, and a metal badge.
>
> After every six months of satisfactory service, half diamond to be sewn on armlet, special armlet after two years' service and scarlet armlet to replace the two-year one after four years.
>
> Every 12 months some uniform replacement – free but surrender some [clothing] coupons.[4]

# Notes

**Dedication**

1 National recruitment leaflet for WLA, 1917.

**Preface and Acknowledgements**

1 Lucy Fisher, *Women in the War* (London: HarperCollins, 2021), p.93.

**1. Introduction**

1 www.visionofbritain.org.uk (accessed 23 July 2023).
2 Report of the sub-committee appointed to consider the employment of women in agriculture in England and Wales (Board of Agriculture and Fisheries, 1919), pp.25 and 117.
3 Ibid, p.119.
4 Lynn Abrams, *Myth and Maternity in a Woman's World* (Manchester: Manchester University Press, 2005), p.15.

**2. Initial National Response to Labour Shortages on Farms**

1 *Hansard* report of a debate held on 22 May 1916 (Vol. 82cc1831–952).
2 *Hansard,* for 20 April 1914 (Vol. 61cc562–3).
3 *Westminster Gazette*, 2 July 1915.
4 *Aberdeen Journal*, 12 June 1915.
5 Gill Clarke, *The Women's Land Army: A Portrait* (Bristol: Sansom & Co Ltd, 2008), pp.11–12.
6 *The Spectator*, 9 June 1916.
7 Gill Clarke, *The Women's Land Army: A Portrait*, p.21.
8 *Hampshire Independent*, 15 January 1916. For most of the first half of the twentieth century there were at least seven local weekly newspapers that served Hampshire's population.
9 *Portsmouth Evening News*, 11 May 1916.
10 *Hampshire Telegraph*, 28 January 1916.
11 *Hampshire Advertiser*, 14 July 1917.

12 *Hampshire Chronicle*, 4 October 1918.
13 *Hampshire Telegraph*, 3 March 1916.
14 *Hampshire Advertiser*, 2 February 1918.
15 Caroline Scott, *Holding the Home Front: The Women's Land Army in the First World War* (Barnsley: Pen & Sword Books Ltd, 2020), p.76.

**3. Hampshire's Responses to Labour Shortages on Farms up to 1916**

1 Minutes of Sparsholt Farm School Special Sub-Committee, 29 March 1915.
2 *Common Cause,* 13 August 1915.
3 *Hampshire Observer and Basingstoke News*, 8 May 1915.
4 For most of the nineteenth century Westley Farm had been owned by the Fitt family. It was sold to Robert Provo Wallis Wilson in 1892. Hampshire County Council bought 251 acres, including Westley House, in 1912 for £5,300, including purchaser's costs.
5 Ibid.
6 Ibid.
7 Ibid.
8 Ibid.
9 *North Devon Journal*, quoting Arthur Marwick, *Women at War 1914–1918*, 'Tales from the Archives', (online journal for the North Devon Athenaeum).
10 *Hampshire Advertiser*, 5 February 1916.
11 War Agricultural Executive Committees ('War Ags'), were government bodies established in the autumn of 1915. Each English county's 'War Ag' was tasked with increasing agricultural production.
12 *Suffolk and Essex Free Press*, 16 May 1900.
13 *Hampshire Observer and Basingstoke News*, 18 December 1915.
14 Gill Clarke, *The Women's Land Army: A Portrait*, p.13.
15 *Hampshire Independent*, 8 April 1916.
16 *Hampshire Independent*, 15 January 1916.
17 Caroline Scott, *Holding the Home Front*, p.64.
18 *Chelmsford Chronicle*, 18 February 1916.
19 *Daily Mirror*, 25 October 1916.
20 *Hampshire Independent*, 19 February 1916.
21 *Hampshire Independent*, 29 June 1916.
22 *Hampshire Observer and Basingstoke News*, 17 April 1915.
23 *Hampshire Independent*, 1 April 1916.
24 Minutes of Sparsholt Farm School Special Sub-Committee, 2 December 1918.
25 *Hampshire Advertiser*, 15 June 1918.
26 www.ancestry.com*; Public Member Stories,* Mary Katherine Cook.
27 Certificate, January 1918, Hampshire Record Office (HRO, 17M81/3).
28 Conversation with Philip White, 8 January 2024. Pauline Woolmer White was Philip's great-aunt.

29 *Hants and Sussex News*, 28 July 1915. A 'shuck' is a 'pile or assemblance of grain'.
30 *Portsmouth Evening News*, 21 March 1916.
31 Nick Baldwin, *Tractors 1880s to 1980s* (Oxford: Shire Publications, 2010), p.15.
32 *Hampshire Advertiser*, 5 December 1914, and *Hampshire Independent*, 14 December 1918. The two other original depots were at Ormskirk and Shirehampton, close to the ports of Liverpool and Avonmouth.
33 www.ltvas.org.uk 'Romsey War Horse and Remount Depot', (Romsey Local History Society), www.swaythling.org.uk 'Swaythling Remount Depot', www.nationalarchives.gov.uk 'Making Horses for War: the Army Remount Service' (article by Sally Hoult, August 2017) (all accessed 20 November 2023). Additional information from Romsey Local History website, article by Pat Genge, 'Horse Power in World War 1', July 1999, and explanatory plaque in Romsey's War Memorial Park.
34 This story was relayed to the author in a conversation with John Marshall on 6 December 2023. Mr Marshall has worked at the Redenham estate for almost fifty years.

**4. The Women's Land Army from March 1917, Nationally and in Hampshire**

1 Much of the material in this chapter comes from a folder held at the Hampshire Record Office headed 'National Service Committee' (HRO; W/C1/5/594) containing posters, letters to and from Winchester City Council officials, and leaflets – all from 1917.
2 *Hampshire Telegraph*, 19 January 1917.
3 *Hampshire Independent*, 6 January 1917.
4 TNA:NATS 1/275, quoted in Teresa Sanders, *A Call to the Women of Great Britain: The Formation of the Women's Land Army* (First World War, Social History, the National Archives), 4 October 2017.
5 *Hampshire Telegraph*, 30 March 1917.
6 *Aldershot News*, 6 April 1917.
7 Leaflet, *National Service Women's Land Army* (Board of Agriculture and Fisheries), 1917.
8 Leaflet W11, 'Why every man should enrol – A Brief for Canvassers', *Waistcoat pocket notes for Speakers*, (National Services Department, 15 March 1917), and letter from the department dated 13 March 1917.
9 Leaflet, NSVT 4.
10 Advertisement, 'The Women's Land Army needs <u>YOU</u> to-day', undated, circa mid-1917.
11 Letter from Arthur Collins, secretary of the National Services Department, 5 July 1917.
12 Undated leaflet, 'Don't Delay – Enrol Today'.
13 Gill Clarke, *The Women's Land Army: A Portrait*, p.30.
14 *Hampshire Advertiser*, 8 June 1918.
15 *The Times*, 21 November 1917, 'The Danger of Food Queues' (HRO, 170A12W/D/4683), p.45.

16 *The Landswoman*, July 1918, p.137.
17 Wikipedia, *U-boat campaign* (accessed 9 July 2023).
18 *The Landswoman*, July 1919, p.171.
19 Draft agreement for tenancy of Lyde Green Farmhouse, Rotherwick, Hampshire, 11 June 1918 (HRO; 63M83/B14/16).
20 *Hampshire Independent*, 10 February 1917 and 16 March 1917.
21 *Birmingham Post*, 3 April 1917.
22 *Isle of Wight Observer*, 16 October 1920.
23 Carol Twinch, *Women on the Land: Their Story During Two World Wars* (Cambridge: Lutterworth Press, 1990), p.16.
24 *The Landswoman*, June 1918, p.136.
25 *Hampshire Telegraph*, 13 December 1929.
26 *Hampshire Telegraph*, 25 January 1918.
27 *Hampshire Telegraph*, 26 April 1918.
28 *Hampshire Advertiser*, 29 June 1918.
29 *Hampshire independent*, 9 February 1918.
30 *Hampshire Advertiser*, 3 March 1917.
31 Gill Clarke, *The Women's Land Army: A Portrait*, 'Occupations of Women in the Land Army, Autumn 1918', p.35.
32 *Hampshire Telegraph*, 3 January 1919.
33 *Hampshire Independent,* 1 June 1918, 6 July 1918 and 3 August 1918.
34 *Hampshire Independent*, 9 March 1918.
35 *Hampshire Independent*, 30 November 1918.
36 *Hampshire Advertiser*, 30 November 1918.
37 www.hampshirewi.org.uk 'WI House – A Brief History' (accessed 1 January 2024).
38 www.sallybosleybadgeshop.com (accessed 2 November 2023).
39 www.womenslandarmy.co.uk – WW1 Handbook.
40 *Hampshire Advertiser*, 2 February 1918.

**5. Post-war Experience**
1 *The Landswoman,* December 1918, quoted in *Hampshire Advertiser,* 29 November 1919.
2 *The Landswoman,* December 1918, p.262.
3 *The Landswoman,* November 1919, p.270.
4 E. Walford Lloyd, *Hampshire Telegraph,* 24 February 1939.
5 Miss Meriel Talbot, letter, 14 October 1919, quoted in Gill Clarke, *The Women's Land Army: A Portrait*, p.58.
6 *Hampshire Independent*, 11 October 1919.
7 *The Landswoman,* May 1919, p.114.
8 *Hampshire Advertiser*, 15 January 1916.
9 *Aldershot News*, 30 May 1919.
10 The National Federation of Discharged Sailors and Soldiers was formed in January 1917, and merged with other bodies in 1921, so establishing the Royal British Legion.
11 *Hampshire Telegraph*, 15 August 1919.

12 *Hampshire Telegraph*, 15 November 1918.
13 *Hampshire Advertiser*, 20 December 1919.
14 *Hampshire Telegraph*, 26 September 1919.
15 *Hampshire Telegraph*, 10 October 1919.
16 *The Landswoman,* August 1919, p.174.
17 Ibid.
18 *Exeter and Plymouth Gazette*, 11 November 1919.
19 *Portsmouth Evening News*, 20 February 1920.
20 *Portsmouth Evening News*, article by Raymond Burns, Political Correspondent, 24 February 1940.

**6. Postscript**

1 www.dailymail.co.uk – Amanda Cable, 'Condemned to be virgins: two million women robbed by war' (*Daily Mail* Online, 15 September 2007).
2 David R. Mace, *Family Life in Britain Since the First World War* (Sage Publications Inc. Annuals of the American Academy of Political Social Science, Vol. 272, 'Towards Family Stability', November 1950), pp.179–184.
3 Sarah Churchwell, 'The Age of Emancipation' (*History Revealed*, March 2023), p.48.
4 encyclopedia:1914-1918-online.net – For a detailed international study of this subject, see Richard Bessel, 'Post-war Societies' (*International Encyclopaedia of the First World War*, 5 December 2017).
5 *Hampshire Advertiser*, 16 September 1939.

**7. Introduction**

1 *Hampshire Telegraph*, 24 February 1939, and *Hampshire Advertiser*, 25 February 1939.
2 For a comprehensive summary of the rationing arrangements, see *History Revealed,* 'Graphic History – 1954, The End of Rationing', January 2024, pp.18 and 19.
3 Quoted in R.J. Moore-Colyer, 'Kids in the Corn: School Harvest Camps and Farm Labour Supply in England, 1940–1950', in *The Agricultural History Review,* January 2004, pp.183–206. Original source, Agricultural Statistics, 1939–1951, Brown, *Agriculture in England*, p.138.
4 *Hampshire Telegraph*, 10 November 1939.
5 *Portsmouth Evening News*, 22 April 1940.

**8. Early Women's Land Army Training at the County Farm Institute, Sparsholt**

1 *Hampshire Advertiser*, 13 May 1939.
2 Minutes of Sparsholt Farm Institute Sub-Committee, 12 June 1939.
3 *Student Register*, 1937 to 1943 (HRO, ref; 100/M95/32).
4 The Quaker Meeting House at Sea Street, Newport, PO40 9PS, is the only one on the Isle of Wight.
5 *Student Register,* 1937 to 1943 (HRO; ref.100M95/32).

6 *Student Register,* 1937 to 1943, and 1943 to 1947 (HRO; refs.100M95/32 and 100M95/33).
7 Gill Clarke, *Evelyn Dunbar, War and Country* (Bristol: Sansom & Co. Ltd, 2006), letter from Michael Greenhill to Gill Clarke, p.87.
8 Evelyn Dunbar was appointed an official war artist by the War Artists' Advisory Committee. Much of her work featured the WLA. In 1942 she married Roger Folley who, for a short time, had been a member of Sparsholt's staff. She died in 1960 after suffering a heart attack when out walking with her husband near their home in Kent.
9 'A Hampshire Service of Thanksgiving to recognise the contribution made by members of The Women's Land Army and Women's Timber Corps', Winchester Cathedral, 7 May 2009, p.7.
10 Christopher Campbell-Howes, *Evelyn Dunbar, An occasional series of commentaries* (August 2012).
11 José Loosemore, *My War: The 'Invasion' of the Hampshire Downs* (BBC – WW2 People's War, December 2003).
12 *Hampshire Advertiser*, 27 April 1940.
13 *Hampshire Advertiser*, '"The Land Army in Training", A Day at the Hampshire Farm Institute, Town Girls Happy in Rural Life', 29 June 1940.
14 John Lander, *A Place of Transformation, The History of Sparsholt College, Hampshire, from 1899* (Portsmouth: Tricorn Books, 2022), p.112.

**9. Women's Land Army Members' Experience in Hampshire, 1939–1942**

1 *Hampshire Telegraph*, 19 January 1940.
2 *Student Register,* 1937–1943, (HRO; ref 100M95/32). The author is grateful to John Parrington, Isabella's son, for providing copies of material the family has retained, and for other information gained during a conversation on 4 January 2024. See Appendix C for two poems written by Isabella Waddell in 1941.
3 Gill Clarke, *The Women's Land Army: A Portrait*, p.66.
4 *Hampshire Telegraph*, 8 August 1941.
5 Anne Hall, *Land Girl: Her Story of Six Years in the Women's Land Army 1940–46* (Bradford on Avon: Ex Libris Press, 1993), pp.23–56.
6 *Hampshire Advertiser*, 13 April 1940.
7 *Hampshire Telegraph*, 24 January 1941.
8 *Hampshire Advertiser*, 20 January 1940.
9 *Hampshire Telegraph*, 21 March 1940.
10 *Hampshire Advertiser*, 20 April 1940.
11 *Hampshire Telegraph*, 24 January 1941.
12 Wording of WLA membership card issued to Miss I.D.S. Waddell, 25 July 1940.
13 *Portsmouth Evening News*, 14 June 1940, and *Hampshire Telegraph*, 21 June 1940.
14 *Portsmouth Evening News*, 8 January 1941, and *Hampshire Telegraph*, 10 January 1941.
15 Conversation with Bruce and Gill Horn, 5 January 2024. 'Bunty' Horniblow was a cousin of Bruce Horn.

16 Letter, Lady Denman to Pauline Woolmer White, 17 September 1941 (HRO ref; 17M81/5).

17 Letter, from G. Denman, Honorary Director of the Women's Land Army, 16 July 1942 (HRO ref; 17M81/6).

18 *Hampshire Telegraph*, 4 July 1941.

19 The author's conversations with Chris Roles, 18 November 2023. Chris's grandfather had a large sheep farm at Dean, a village between Romsey and Salisbury.

20 Kesby (Bob) Horn, [working title] *The Life of a Hampshire Farmer*, p.7 (book in process of being written by Kesby Horn, a grandson of Bob Horn). The author appreciated the opportunity to spend an afternoon with Gill, Bruce and Kesby Horn at their farm in Meonstoke, 5 January 2024.

21 Handwritten note by Miss Pauline Woolmer White, 'Notes on interviewing girls who wish to join the Women's Land Army', undated, probably 1942 (HRO ref; 17M81/29).

22 Ibid.

23 There are many books giving the service details of WLA members; for example, Anne Hall, *Land Girl*, pp.71–84.

24 List of committee members, representatives and the hostels and their areas of responsibility (HRO ref; 17M81/35) and 'Notes on the duties of District or Parish representatives' (17M81/32).

25 *Hampshire Telegraph*, 22 August 1941.

26 Building plan for 'Agricultural Workers' Hostel' (HRO ref; 39M73/BP4236).

27 *The Land Girl*, October 1942, Vol. 3, No. 7, p.14.

28 The Redenham Estate Andover Hampshire – Auction 1948, p.9. The auction took place on 3 September 1948, and was bought for £57,000 by a John Read. (Information from John Marshall, 13 December 2023.)

29 Ibid, pp.6–8.

30 *Andover Advertiser*, 13 September 1946.

31 Victoria Panton Bacon, *Remarkable Women of the Second World War* (Cheltenham: The History Press, 2022), pp.59, 64–67; www.womenslandarmy.co.uk re. Gwendoline Yvonne Raggett (née Place), WW2 Profile, and a conversation between the author and Gwen and her daughter in law (Heather Raggett), 20 December 2023. Additional information provided by John Marshall on 6 and 12 December, who has worked for the Redenham estate for almost fifty years. The plaque remains in place, cared for by John Marshall.

32 www.womenslandarmy.co.uk re. Redenham House. Profile of Betty Dannatt (née Wellings) (accessed 2 November 2023).

33 www.history@woodgreenshop.org, 'Hale Nursery – House of Flowers', 2007. The housing, built in the 1990s, is now Dodgson Close, Wood Green, Fordingbridge (accessed 4 October 2023).

34 'Hostel "House Rules"', undated, probably 1940 or 1941 (HRO ref; 17M81/34).

35 'Notes on the duties of Hostel Representatives' (HRO ref; 17M81/30).

36 Nancy Cooper, *Down to Earth* (Studeley, Warwickshire: Brewin Books Ltd, 2017), p.20.
37 Anonymous copy memoir, (HRO ref; COPY868/1).
38 *Hampshire Advertiser*, 20 April 1940.
39 *Hampshire Telegraph*, 12 January 1940.
40 *Portsmouth Evening News*, 6 January 1940.
41 *Portsmouth Evening News*, 18 April 1942.
42 *Chester Chronicle*, 13 June 1942.
43 Quoted in *Portsmouth Evening News,* 4 January 1940.
44 Barbara Curtis, *Fresh Air, A Childhood in Portchester and a Land Army Girl* (Hampshire Rose Books, 2003), p.32.
45 *Portsmouth Evening News*, 9 January 1940.
46 *Hampshire Telegraph*, 27 November 1940.
47 *Portsmouth Evening News*, 21 February 1941.
48 *Portsmouth Evening News*, 12 December 1941.
49 Gill Clarke, *The Women's Land Army: A Portrait*, p.89.
50 V. Sackville-West, *The Women's Land Army* (London: Michael Joseph Ltd, 1944), p.82.
51 Sheila Blatch, 'My Experience in the WLA, 1942–1950' (HRO ref; 193A09/1).
52 Notes entitled 'The Farmer's Calendar of Work' (HRO ref; 17M81/38).

**10. Expansion of Women's Land Army in Hampshire, 1943–1945**

1 *Hampshire Telegraph*, 21 April 1944.
2 Conversation with Gwen Raggett, 20 December 2023.
3 Kesby (Bob) Horn, *The Life of a Hampshire Farmer*, p.7 (book in process of being written by Kesby Horn, a grandson of Bob Horn).
4 Anne Hall, *Land Girl*, pp.37–38.
5 *Hampshire Telegraph*, 13 October 1944.
6 *Portsmouth Evening News*, 5 June 1942 and 29 April 1943.
7 *Portsmouth Evening News*, 17 April 1943, and www.womenslandarmy.co.uk, 'Women's Land Army and Timber Corps' (accessed 4 October 2023).
8 Various contributors, *'Meet the Members', A Record of the Timber Corps of the Women's Land Army* (Home Production Department, Ministry of Supply, 1945), pp.64–65. Profits from the sale of the book were to be given to the WLA Benevolent Fund. The Barton Stacey Rifle Range, now known as Moody's Down Range, is 1 mile south of Barton Stacey village. It remains a military shooting training centre.
9 Op. cit; quoted in R.J. Moore-Colyer, pp.192–202.
10 *Daily News (London)*, 27 September 1943.
11 *Daily News (London)*, 27 September 1943. The episode involving Amelia King appeared in many newspapers in October and November 1943, including *Daily Mirror*, 9 October; *Birmingham Daily Mail*, 27 October; *Yorkshire Evening Post*, 8 October; *Taunton Courier, and Western Advertiser,* 30 October, and *Lincolnshire Echo*, 8 October.

12 Article by Kirsten Robertson, 'Amelia King: The woman barred from aiding Britain's WW2 efforts because she was Black', *Metro*, 6 October 2023.
13 Learie Constantine, born in Trinidad, became a famous West Indian cricketer but, with his family, was refused accommodation at a London hotel in 1943 because of the colour of his skin.
14 *Revised Conditions for Applicants*, December 1943 (Ministry of Agriculture and Fisheries) (HRO ref; 108A03/9/1).
15 Letter, 29 June 1945 (HRO ref; 108A03/9/5).
16 Brooksby Hall Training Centre, Leicestershire, was established especially for ex-servicemen, and was one of at least nine land-based institutions set up during or soon after the Second World War. In the southern half of England they included Kingston Maurward, Dorchester, Bicton Farm Institute, South Devon and Hartpury, Gloucestershire.
17 *Hampshire Telegraph*, 15 September 1944.
18 *Portsmouth Evening News*, 13 April 1944.
19 *Hampshire Telegraph*, 15 June 1945.
20 *Hampshire Telegraph*, 8 September 1944.
21 Professor David Reynolds, 'Who was Winston Churchill's closest advisor?' (*BBC History Revealed*, December 2023), p.62.
22 *Portsmouth Evening News*, 10 December 1942.
23 *Hampshire Telegraph*, 25 May 1945.
24 www.womenslandarmy.co.uk.
25 www.womenslandarmy.co.uk, Benevolent Fund, Bulletin 1, June 1943.
26 www.womenslandarmy.co.uk, Benevolent Fund, Bulletin 3, May 1944.
27 *The Land Girl,* October 1942, Vol. 3, No. 7.
28 *Hampshire Telegraph*, 25 February 1944.
29 V. Sackville-West, *The Women's Land Army* (London: Michael Joseph Ltd, 1944), p.84.
30 *Hampshire Telegraph*, 2 November 1945.
31 *Hampshire Telegraph*, 23 February 1945.
32 Quoted in www.womenslandarmy.co.uk>world-war-two.
33 *Hampshire Telegraph*, 19 January 1945.
34 Gold Certificate, 8 May 1945 (HRO; 17M81/4).
35 Letter, 29 June 1945, (HRO ref; 108A03/9/6).
36 Letter, 6 June 1946, (HRO ref; 108A03/9/7).
37 Letter, 29 June 1946.
38 *Hampshire Telegraph*, 2 November 1945.
39 *Hampshire Telegraph*, 5 July 1946.
40 Letter, November 1945 (HRO ref; 50M90/1).
41 *Hampshire Telegraph*, 23 February 1945.
42 *Hampshire Telegraph*, 13 April 1945.
43 *Hampshire Telegraph*, 23 February 1945.
44 *Hampshire Telegraph*, 18 May 1945.

45 *Hampshire Telegraph*, 18 May 1945.
46 *Hampshire Telegraph*, 12 April 1946.

**11. Continuing Role for Women's Land Army After 1945**

1 www.westminster-abbey.org re. VE Day (accessed 10 September 2023).
2 www.culturaloncall.com, 'Victory Celebration in Aldershot, May 1945', quoted from article by Paul Vickers, Chair, Aldershot Military Museum (Hampshire Cultural Trust).
3 *Hampshire Observer and County Newspaper and General Advertiser*, 18 August 1945.
4 *New Milton Advertiser*, 5 January 1946.
5 *Hampshire Telegraph*, 5 April 1946.
6 *Hampshire Telegraph*, 21 June 1946.
7 *New Milton Advertiser*, 10 May 1947.
8 *New Milton Advertiser*, 19 April 1947.
9 *Hampshire Telegraph*, 10 October 1948.
10 *Hampshire Telegraph*, 28 May 1948.
11 Letters dated 3 February 1948 and 6 February 1948 (HRO Ref; 17M81/17 and 18).
12 Elizabeth Bridges, *I'd Almost Forgotten That!* (undated, *c.* 1997), and email, 12 December 2020. The author is grateful to Elizabeth Bridges who, well into her nineties, held a fascinating conversation with him at her home on 25 October 2022. Sadly, she died in August 2023.
13 Elizabeth Bridges, 'Elizabeth Bridges' Memories of the Land Army and beyond', paper attached to a letter to the author dated 11 November 2022, pp.2–5.
14 Brown, 'Agriculture in England: Agriculture Statistics, 1939–1951' (*The Agricultural History Review*, January 2004), p.138, quoted in R.J. Colyer-Moore, 'Kids in the Corn: School Harvest Camps and Farm Labour Supply in England, 1940–1950'.
15 Circular letter dated July 1947 (HRO Ref; 17M81/16).
16 *Hampshire Telegraph*, 8 December 1950.
17 Speech by Her Majesty the Queen, *Journal of the Ministry of Agriculture*, Vol. 57, No. 9, December 1950, p.401.
18 *The Land Girl*, final bulletin, Vol. V1, No. 6, November 1950.
19 *Portsmouth Evening News*, 7 February 1950.
20 *Portsmouth Evening News*, 18 October 1950.
21 Dr E. Gordon Selwyn was born in Liverpool, the son of Edward Selwyn, a Church of England clergyman who later became headmaster of Uppingham School, and his wife, Lucy. Rev. John P. Boden was born at Sithney, near Helston, Cornwall, the son of Frederick Boden, a Wesleyan Methodist minister, and his wife, Mary. The text of the hymn is given in Appendix A – the tune used was 'Epiphany'.
22 *Portsmouth Evening News*, 20 February 1951.
23 *The Dorset County Chronicle and Somersetshire Gazette*, 4 May 1968 (HRO refs; 50M90/11, 50M90/13).

24 Letter, from Miss Diane Darling, County Secretary of the Federation of Hampshire Women's Institutes (HRO ref: 51M97/C1/8).
25 Ibid.
26 Invoice, 16 September 1943; Receipt, 21 September 1943 (HRO ref; 17M81/8).
27 Letter to NFU, 18 February 1965 (HRO ref;17M81/26), replies 1 March 1965 and 4 March 1965 (HRO ref: 17M81/27 and 28). Regrettably, the current whereabouts of the banner is unknown.
28 *New Milton Advertiser*, 15 June 1996.
29 'A Hampshire Service of Thanksgiving to recognise the contribution of The Women's Land Army and Women's Timber Corps', Winchester Cathedral, 7 May 2009.

**12. Conclusion**

1 V. Sackville-West, *The Women's Land Army*, Appendix 1.
2 Gill Clarke, *The Women's Land Army: A Portrait*, p.8.
3 *The Independent*, 28 January 2008.
4 Kirsty Thorpe, 'For Woman and Man a Place at the Table' (*The Journal of the United Reformed Church History Society*, 2023), Vol. 11 No. 3, November 2023, p.137.

**Appendices**

1 The author was privileged to have an in-depth conversation with Gwen and her daughter-in-law, Heather Raggett, on 20 December 2023.
2 Email to the author from Heather Raggett, 9 January 2024.
3 The author is extremely grateful to Gwen and Heather Raggett, who willingly provided information, copies of documents, and photographs that the family has retained.
4 V. Sackville-West, *The Women's Land Army*, Appendix 9, p.105.

# Bibliography


Abrams, Lynn, *Myth and Maternity in a Woman's World* (Manchester: Manchester University Press, 2005)

Bacon, Victoria Panton, *Remarkable Women of the Second World War: A Collection of Untold Stories* (Cheltenham: The History Press, 2022)

Baldwin, Nick, *Tractors 1880s to 1980s* (Oxford: Shire Publications, 2010)

Bridges, Elizabeth, *I'd Almost Forgotten That!* (self-published, circa 1997)

Butler, Simon, *Land Girl Suffragette: The Extraordinary Story of Olive Hockin* (Wellington, Somerset: Halstar Ltd, 2016)

Clarke, Gill, *Evelyn Dunbar, War and Country* (Bristol: Sansom & Co. Ltd, 2006)

Clarke, Gill, *The Women's Land Army: A Portrait* (Bristol: Sansom & Co Ltd, 2008)

Cooper, Nancy, *Down to Earth: Memories of a young woman joining the Women's Land Army in 1943* (Studeley: Brewin Books Ltd, 2017)

Curtis, Barbara, *Fresh Air: A Childhood in Portchester and a Land Army Girl* (Hampshire Rose Books, 2003)

Fisher, Lucy, *Women in the War* (London: HarperCollins, 2021)

Hall, Anne, *Land Girl: Her Story of Six Years in the Women's Land Army, 1940–46* (Bradford-on-Avon: Ex Libris Press, 1993)

Horn, Kesby (Bob), *The Life of a Hampshire Farmer* (working title of a book being written)

Lander, John, *A Place of Transformation: The History of Sparsholt College, Hampshire, from 1899* (Portsmouth: Tricorn Books, 2022)

Mace, David R., *Family Life in Britain Since the First World War: Towards Family Stability* (Sage Publications Inc., November 1950)

Moore-Colyer, R.J., 'Kids in the Corn: School Harvest Camps and farm labour supply in England, 1940–1950', *The Agricultural History Review* (British Agricultural History Society, 1988)

Ross, Patricia, *Hampshire at War: An Oral History, 1939–1945* (Huddersfield: The King's English Press, 2013)

Rushton, Gillian A., *100 Years of Progress: Hampshire County Council 1889–1989* (Winchester: Hampshire County Council, 1989)

Sackville-West, V., *The Women's Land Army* (London: Michael Joseph Ltd, 1944)

Scott, Caroline, *Holding the Home Front: The Women's Land Army in the First World War* (Barnsley: Pen and Sword Books Ltd, 2017)

Storey, Neil R. and Kay, Fiona, *Women in the Second World War* (Stroud: Amberley Publishing, 2019)

Twinch, Carol, *Women on the Land: Their Story During Two World Wars* (Cambridge: Lutterworth Press, 1990)

White, Bonnie, *The Women's Land Army in First World War Britain* (Basingstoke: Palgrave MacMillan, 2014)

Wynn, Stephen and Wynn, Tanya, *Women in the Great War* (Barnsley: Pen and Sword Books Ltd, 2017)

Various contributors, *Meet the Members: A Record of the Timber Corps of the Women's Land Army* (London: Home Timber Production Dept, Ministry of Supply, 1945)

# Index


Acland, Francis Dyke MP 23
Agricultural Education Conference, December 1914 21, 26
Agriculture – employees to armed forces 20, 21, 24, 32, 59, 70, 82, 104
Recession 57, 58, 60
Aldershot 109
Anderson, Capt. Oswald 70
Andover 45, 107, 108
Astor, Nancy (Viscountess) 61

Barr, Maureen (see De Rougemont)
Bartlett, Sue M. 61
Benn, Arthur MP 43
Bevin, Ernest MP 101
Biggs, E.M. 79
Bishop's Waltham 88
Board of Agriculture 21, 35, 37, 39, 51
Boden, Rev. John P 115
Botley 88
Bournemouth High School for Girls 59
Bridges, Elizabeth (née Cheal) 15, 111–12
Britles, Miss 74
Broadbent, Margaret 29
Bullock, E.J. 74

Campbell, Patricia 99
Christian, Thomas 46
Churcher, Miss 44
Churchill, Clementine Ogilvy Spencer 104
Winston 109
Chute, Sir Charles 67, 76
Lady Laura J 33, 67, 76, 79, 81
Chute Standen 88, 89
Colden Common, Brambridge 87
Conscientious objectors 53, 70, 98
Cooper, Nancy 93
Cook, Mary Kathleen (Kitty) 33, 51
Cowan, David T. 25–26

Dannatt, Betty (née Wellings) 91
Darling, Diana 116
Darrell, Mary 29, 31
Davidson, J. Duncan 27, 30
Denham, P. 107
Denman, Gertrude (Baroness) 49, 76, 81, 101, 106, 108
De Rougemont, Maureen 78–79
Dodgson, Capt. Guy 91
Dorman-Smith, Reginald MP 76
Drake-Brockman, Moyra 89
Dudgeon, Mrs 57
Dulwich College 78
Dunbar, Evelyn 73, 87

Edwards, Walter MP 101
Emergency Land Corps 94

Fagan, Mary 118
Folley, Roger 73
Food Control Committee 47
  Rationing 46, 47, 57, 65, 66
Freshfield, Agnes C. 34
  Jessie 34

German U-boats 40, 44
Gidley, Sandra MP 61
Gleed, Charles J. 30
Greenhill, Michael 73
Griffiths, E. Kenneth 116

Haigh, Rev. Mervyn 114
Hale Nursery, Fordingbridge 91, 92
Hall, Anne 76
Hambledon, Hipley Farm 82
Hampshire, County Council 25, 70
  Farm School 25, 26, 27, 47
  War Agricultural Executive Committee 28, 33, 38, 43, 75, 78, 111
Hanan, Thelma 106
Havant 106
Haymaking 112
Hill, Thomas H. 37
Hook 88
Horn family 82, 98
Horniblow, Kathleen (Bunty) 80
Horses 20, 35, 48
Horticulture 19, 30, 47, 72, 74, 79, 84, 91, 98, 102, 109, 118
Hostels 33, 44, 58, 84, 86–88, 91–93, 98, 113–14
Hudson, Robert MP 95, 97, 101
Huskisson, Olive C. 106–07, 111
'Hymn of the Hampshire Countryside' 115

Imports of food 24, 40, 43, 44
Independent Agricultural Parliamentary Party 46
Isle of Wight 32, 39, 44, 54, 94

Keable, Doreen 99
Keenleyside, W.J. 116
King, Amelia 100–02
Kingsclere 88
King's Somborne 80

Lambley, John R. 108
Land Army Resettlement Scheme 56
Lee, Arthur MP (Viscount) 34, 52
Leeson, Canon Spencer 78
Liphook 105
Liss 116
Lloyd George, David MP 44
Loosemore, Jose 73
Lyttleton, Edith (Dame) 51

Madeley, Martha 115
Marshall, John 91
Meonstoke, Pondside Farm 98
Meyer, Rev. Frederick B. 52
Miles, Frank 111
Military Services Bill, 1916 24
Milkers 27, 31, 40, 47, 55, 70, 73, 82, 114
Moore, R.T. 107
Mottisfont 106

National Arboretum, Alrewas, Staffordshire 121
National Association of Landswomen 57
National Farmers' Union 53, 66, 77, 79, 91, 94, 98, 104, 109, 116
National Federation of Discharged Sailors and Soldiers 55
National Union of Agricultural Workers 95, 108
National Union of Teachers 30
National Union of Women Teachers 29
New Milton 105, 118
Northbrook, Florence (Countess) 31, 49
Norway 40, 99

Old Basing 26

Palmer, William MP 38
Perrott, Gertrude 44, 45, 54
Petersfield 34, 38, 61
Portsmouth 46, 95, 111
Prisoners of War 53, 66, 82, 98, 110
Prothero, Rowland MP (1st Baron Emle) 24, 25, 38, 39, 40, 52

Quennell, Joan MP 61

Raggett, Gwendoline Y. (Gwen) (née Place) 15, 89
Redenham House and Estate 37, 88–91
Register, 1939 68, 69
Roberts, Alfred E. 101–02
Romsey 33, 48, 61
  Horse Remount Depot 35, 36
Rowland Castle 106
Royal School of Needlework 116

School Release Scheme 99–100
Selborne, Earl (see Palmer, William) 22, 23
Selwyn, Dr E. Gordon 115
Sherborne St John 44
Slade, Olive 107
Smith, Frederick 44
Smith, Ronald Harris 69, 70
Southampton 47, 95, 106, 109
  Regent's Park School 78
Spanish flu 59
Sparsholt Farm Institute 11, 15, 20, 67, 68, 70, 73, 94, 97, 104, 111, 115
Stockbridge 75, 78, 80, 88
Strawberries 78, 79
Sugar beet 79
Swanwick and District Fruit Growers' Association 98
Swaythling Horse Remount Depot 35

Talbot, Meriel 40, 53
Thatching 47, 55, 74, 77
*The Land Girl* 105, 114
*The Landswoman* 52, 56
Thomas, David A. MP (Viscount Rhondda) 46
Threshing 76, 79
Titchfield. 105
Tredwell, E. Jack 73
Troup, Major Lindsay G. 68, 69, 78
Tugwell, Rev. Lewen 53

Unemployment 60
Upham 74, 76, 78

Veniscombe House, Newchurch, Isle of Wight 44, 45
Volunteer Agricultural Camps 78

Waddell, Isabella D.S. 75, 80
War Pensions Committee 45, 67
Warsash 55
War Work for Women Committee 31, 32, 33
Waterlooville 35
Westley Farm, Sparsholt 26, 97
Wickham, Frith Farm 102
Williams, Tom MP 110
Williamson, Carolyn 61
Winchester Cathedral 109, 114–15, 118–19
  City Council 43, 47
  College 38, 78
  Rural District Council 49, 86, 87
Women Farm employees 11, 19, 20, 27, 32, 39
Women's Defence League Corps 22
  Farm and Garden Union 22
  Institute 49, 74, 108, 116–18
  Land Army – Agriculture section 47
    Benevolent Fund 104, 106, 113

Clothing 50, 51, 95–96, 108, 118, 120
Foraging Corps 48
Formation 39, 65
Hours of working 48, 60, 76, 84, 95, 102
Numbers 23, 39, 45, 47, 53, 57, 65, 66, 68, 69, 73, 75, 76, 78, 93, 97, 98, 112, 120–21
Old Girls' Association 115–17
Post-wars' farming experience 55, 104, 107
Reluctance to accept WLA members 23, 30, 31, 53, 94, 95
Selection process 40, 41, 45, 84, 100–02
Social class 27, 28, 41, 49, 69
Timber Corps (Second World War) 99
Timber Forestry Corps (First World War) 48, 77
Wages 23, 32, 33, 49, 51, 95, 99, 102, 112
Women's National Land Services Corps 22
Women's Royal Voluntary Service 91, 116
Woolmer White, Pauline 34, 67, 82, 84, 106, 111, 115, 116
Wroth, William H. 80

Young Farmers' Club 79, 112
Young, Harold 73
Youth [Junior] Land Army 45, 94